Teaching with Technology

Teaching with Technology

Integrating Technology into the TESOL Classroom

David Kent

National Library of Australia Cataloguing-in-Publication entry:
Kent, David Bradley, author.
Teaching with technology : integrating technology into the TESOL classroom / David Kent.

ISBN: 9781925555134 (paperback)
Includes bibliographical references.
Teachers of English to Speakers of Other Languages.
Presentation graphics software.
Teaching—Aids and devices.
Educational technology.
Digital storytelling—Study and teaching.
English language—Study and teaching—Foreign speakers.

Pedagogy Press. Sydney, Australia.
www.pedagogypress.com

First Edition.

DEDICATION

For HyunHee.

CONTENTS

ACKNOWLEDGMENTS

I wish to extend my deepest appreciation to my wife *Hyunhee* who has been very patient and understanding throughout the entire process involved with the writing and producing of this book. I would also like to thank *Noel David* for his suggestions and patience. This book would not have been written without him.

PREFACE

Technological advancement is rapid, and its impact on teaching and learning is ever constant. This leads to a need for educators to continually assess and consider the implication that new and emerging technologies may hold for their teaching context, their professional development, and the skills possessed and required by their students. This is where the value of this book becomes apparent, as practitioners will be able to walk away with a greater understanding of how to best employ various aspects of technology-driven learning, instruction, and assessment techniques when teaching English to speakers of other languages (TESOL) from a variety of pedagogical contexts.

1. Introduction

1. Introduction

Since the turn of the century, emerging technologies, along with their use in educational contexts, have seen a number of radical changes occur within the learner landscape, and these have impacted both teachers and students. For English Language Learners, as Goh (2015) recognizes, this has seen changes in the ways that learners engage with content and interact with instructors. Days of the tape-based language lab and the isolated language learner are long gone. Students no longer ask how to pronounce a word, word definitions, or for grammar examples; they can now find these online. Most online dictionaries not only allow for easy access to the definitions, but speak the words as well. Tapes have been replaced with podcasts, YouTube videos, and MP3s for individuals, and with CDs and DVDs in many classrooms. Digital textbooks are being delivered alongside online tutoring and just-in-time learning. There is an ever-increasing availability and access to content, perhaps too much, with quality hard to assess. There are also many literacies to learn – digital literacy, computer literacy, media literacy, information literacy, technology literacy, political literacy, cultural literacy, critical literacy, multicultural literacy, biliteracy, global literacy, and visual literacy to name just a handful. All of this affords learners with increased availability and access to technologies that can augment their exposure to content in many different ways. In other words, learning opportunities have become increasingly interactive, social, and multimodal (Richards, 2014). This, of course, has also seen the way that instructors must teach, provide, and assess content, interact with their students, engage with resources, and develop their craft change as well. Examples here include: flipping the classroom; applying bring-your-own-device (BYOD); integrating app use and normalizing technological use; working with digital textbooks and digitizing story times; developing increasingly visual- and multimedia-focused presentations; engaging in computer-mediated communication (CMC) by constructing visually-based digital conversations both synchronously and asynchronously; providing online tutoring; emailing reports; and relying on just-in-time downloads for classroom activities; developing data driven learning by engaging in aspects of concordancing and vocab profiling; becoming increasingly exposed to social media along with cloud-based learning and teaching techniques; and coping with the gamification of learning and the student need for coding skills – all this while developing online virtual personal learning environments (PLEs). Along with these changes has also come the rise and reliance on social media, accompanied by an ever-increasing use of technology to assist learners with their language skill development.

Organization of the Book

Teaching with Technology aims to cover the use and applicability of various technologies and applications specifically for instructors who are teaching English to speakers of other languages (TESOL) in English as a foreign language (EFL) environments, and it is also worthwhile to any English as a second language (ESL) teacher. In this book, subtitled *Integrating Technology into the TESOL Classroom*, the use of more 'traditional' software tools and classroom staples are reexamined for educational advantage in the digital era and for use with 21st century learners.

The book is intended to be read as a whole or in part, and by teachers, students, parents, or any other stakeholders who may be interested in the topics. Each chapter follows a similar layout, and begins with a short overview in order to situate topics. The overview is followed by a discussion of the relevance of the topic to the wider context of education, prior to presenting the aspects that make that topic effective. How the topic can best be applied in the teaching of English to speakers of other languages (TESOL) context is then introduced, along with a means to evaluate any learner-developed content that may result. Methods for developing effective implementation of the topic are then explored at length before finalizing the chapter with key points. In line with this, each chapter focuses on a single technology topic, and is designed around a question-based format, similar to that outlined here:

- Overview
- What is … ?
- How can I use … ?
- What types of … exist?
- What elements are behind an effective … ?
- How can … lend itself to TESOL?
- How can I start using … with students?
- How do I evaluate a … ?
- What tools are available for … creation?
- How do I craft a … ?
- How would I use a tool to create a … ?
- What are the key points behind … use in the TESOL context?

Chapter One provides the rationale for today's teachers' need of the book, and it lays out the organization of the text. *Chapter Two* presents various methods that engage students in the practice and development of multimedia skills while building their digital literacy and allowing them to make meaning from experience as they construct digital stories from their life cache. *Chapter Three,* by focusing on the Prezi presentation paradigm, highlights the means of creating engaging and interactive multimedia-based presentations that are supportive of a visual, non-linear flow, while *Chapter Four* presents a means of supporting and supplementing instruction through the use of podcasts and screencasts.

Lesson plan guides, example implementation techniques, and various free-to-use handouts for both instructors and their students alike are included in *Chapters Five and Six*. A comprehensive list of resources, with links to pertinent web sites and applications, can be found in *Chapter Seven*. A reference list of all works cited is given in *Chapter Eight*, and it allows teachers to engage in further reading on the issues that most interest them and impact their students.

It is hoped that this book will provide both education and something new for all teachers – be they trained or untrained, pre-service, in-service, seasoned, or retired.

2. Making Meaning from Experience: Digital Storytelling

2. Making Meaning from Experience: Digital Storytelling

Overview

Digital storytelling clearly stands out as an exciting and captivating approach to use for both the teaching and practice of digital literacy, media literacy, and visual literacy skills. The exciting potential behind its use in the teaching of English to speakers of other languages (TESOL) is its ability to give a voice to those students who might come and sit quietly in class and rarely have a chance to speak. Success with digital stories therefore comes when students are empowered with the ability to talk about and make meaning from their life experiences.

This chapter focuses on the use and applicability of digital storytelling in the TESOL context by presenting various methods that can engage students in the practice and development of multimedia skills, while building their digital literacy and allowing them to make meaning from experience as they construct digital stories from their life cache. Attention is placed on the types and effectiveness of digital storytelling, along with constructive means for evaluating student-produced content. A hands-on look at the digital storytelling process provides a practitioner guide, and this is then reinforced with a variety of useful resources to assist both students and teachers alike in getting started with digital storytelling.

What is digital storytelling?

Digital storytelling is the art of combining the skill of storytelling with a mixture of digital graphics, text, audio narration, video, and music (Ohler, 2008), and so the story is therefore primarily a visual one. Digital storytelling scripts are often first person narratives that tell the story in one's own voice and one's own style. As such, each story tends to revolve around a particular theme and contains a single viewpoint that is presented in two to three minutes. The essential challenge that digital storytelling poses to teachers is that of engaging students in the meaningful use of digital imaging (Robin & Pierson, 2005), and seeing students use digital imaging as a mode of communication and for personal reflection (Jenkins & Lonsdale, 2007); in other words, developing learner multimedia literacy levels while guiding students in making meaning from experience.

How can I use digital storytelling?

Digital storytelling essentially allows students to practice multimedia literacy skills. As such, educators in all teaching contexts can employ digital storytelling in a multitude of ways, from introducing new material to assist students in learning to conduct research, through to synthesizing large amounts of content and gaining expertise in the use of digital communication and authoring tools. Instructor created digital stories can also be deployed as a lesson hook, a way to integrate multimedia into the curriculum, to assist in making difficult or complex content more easily understood, or to serve as a jump point for facilitating classroom discussion (Robin, 2008). Student created digital stories, on the other hand, can come to assist learners with idea organization as they begin to develop stories for an audience, and present their ideas and knowledge in uniquely meaningful, individual, and personal ways (Bull & Kajder, 2004). Of course, challenges for students can and do arise, and they range from difficulties in formulating a sound argument through to learners holding low interest in storytelling. Aspects of the digital divide may also see some students having limited access to the appropriate hardware and software to work with digital storytelling dissemination and development. Other students may simply not possess adequate multimedia literacy skills to develop a digital story. Further, content creation with digital storytelling can be time-consuming, and students and teachers who embark on this endeavor need to be well versed in educational fair-use policies, along with the copyright and intellectual issues pertaining to digital content creation and dissemination (Robin, 2008).

What types of digital storytelling exist?

Robin (2008) identifies several different types of digital storytelling, including:

Personal narratives

These are character stories, stories about significant life events, stories about what we do, or any other kind of personal stories like discovery stories, love stories, and recovery stories.

Historical themes and events

These are more than electronic encyclopedia entries; such stories should aim to become engaging and insightful mini-digital documentaries.

Stories that inform or instruct

All digital stories inform or instruct. However, the distinction for this type of digital story is that it is specifically created to deliver learning content, which can cover all academic fields from maths through to medicine.

What elements are behind an effective digital story?

It is important for teachers to assist students in creating digital stories that are effective. The Center for Digital Storytelling (CDS, 2016), along with Lambert (2010), outlines seven key elements that combine to form an effective digital story: point of view, dramatic question, emotional content, economy, pacing, gift of voice, and soundtrack.

Point of view

As digital stories are constructed from students' own experiences and understanding, an embedded point of view in a story comes to successfully establish power of expression for the writer.

Dramatic question

A single dramatic question can serve to hold the attention of the audience throughout the telling of a digital story. However, the question must be answered by the conclusion of the story.

Emotional content

Good stories elicit some kind of emotional response from the audience, like laughter, joy, tears, or surprise. Emotional responses draw an audience in, and allow them to connect to the story.

Economy

Script economy is perhaps one of the most difficult elements of digital storytelling to perform well. Digital stories are concise and are normally two to three minutes in length (about one double-spaced page of text). Particular emphasis on this aspect in educational settings may make the construction process more manageable for learners.

Pacing

Pacing of speech is important. The pausing and varying of speech rhythms are essential to avoid monotony.

Gift of voice

This aspect of digital storytelling, the gift of voice, is one of the most important for language classrooms. Many teachers have those unheard students who are seen entering, submitting work, and leaving at the sound of the bell, but not participating in discussion, group activities, or any task that asks for their verbal participation. The process of digital storytelling allows these students to record themselves verbally narrating their own scripts, and if they are still too shy to speak, the process uniquely allows them to voice their opinions through text titles, highlighting their opinions and presenting their voice in 'silent movie' style.

An accompanying soundtrack

A well chosen and well timed accompanying soundtrack is extremely important. Music can enhance and underscore aspects of a digital story by adding additional layers of complexity and depth to the narrative.

As a point of note here, Robin (2016) would see these seven elements increased to ten within the educational context, adding aspects such as the use of grammar and language, the overall purpose of the story, and the quality of media elements chosen.

How can digital storytelling lend itself to TESOL?

For digital stories to be effective in the TESOL context, it is important that teachers and students focus on different aspects. Teachers can use digital storytelling as a presentation media appealing to diverse learning styles, to generate interest in topics, call attention to a subject, motivate learners, and capitalize on the imaginative talent of students as they start researching and telling their own stories. Students can develop communicative skills by asking questions, expressing opinions, constructing narratives, and writing for an audience. Collaboration of learners in story construction can see summary reports evolve into communication products, with authentic application for the lessons learned in class. Students will also increase their computer skills, and utilize software that combines a variety of media elements including text, still images, audio, and video.

How can I start using digital storytelling with students?

The process of digital storytelling assists with developing several language skills such as reading and writing when storyboarding, and speaking and listening during collaboration and narration. It can also assist in enlarging vocabulary. When working in groups, students are able to share ideas, collaborate on picture selection, communicate, and engage in unique authentic experiences that can transform their understanding of text, words, and images.

A number of traditional TESOL classroom tasks and activities can also easily be transferred to the digital storytelling setting, and they involve: retelling, process writing, portfolio development, and even the digitization of the classroom photo wall. Activities that are well-suited to digital storytelling involve movie trailer development, simulated news broadcasts, product advertising commercials, oral history and re-enactment projects, and virtual tours of schools or cities. Essentially, a great number of classroom tasks or activities can be spiced up with a digital storytelling twist, depending upon the willingness, creativity, and imagination of both the teacher and the students.

How do I evaluate a digital story?

Perhaps the most appropriate means available to evaluate a digital story, particularly in the TESOL context, is to use a prefabricated rubric based upon a Likert-type rating scale. Any such rubric should be presented to students beforehand, so they can understand what will be assessed and expected from them.

Evaluation rubrics, particularly those using indicators across several categories, are essential when assessing the quality of student work on any complex multimedia-based project. Although it is useful for the busy teacher to apply pre-made rubrics, it is even better if teachers formulate ones of their own, so that such rubrics can reflect their teaching environment and the points they wish to assess. One good source for this is Rubistar, where there are a number of pre-made evaluation options as well as information on how to create unique context sensitive evaluation instruments. The rubrics section of the resources list also contains several other rubric creation tools that may prove worthwhile to look over.

The rating scale used in the following rubric goes from 1 to 5, with 1 being poor, 2 fair, 3 average, 4 good, and 5 excellent. 'Average' is used as a midpoint so that students can see how each particular skill relates to peers. This allows teachers to identify those skills that are weak in individual students, and those that may need improvement.

Assessment Item	Assessment Criteria	Score
Point of View/Purpose	Establish a purpose early on, and maintain a clear focus throughout.	1 2 3 4 5
Voice/Pacing	Rhythm and voice fit the story line, and help the audience to get into the story.	1 2 3 4 5
Images	Images create a distinct atmosphere and tone, and aid in communicating symbolism and metaphor.	1 2 3 4 5
Economy	The story is told with the right amount of detail throughout – it does not seem too short or too long.	1 2 3 4 5
Language Use	Language use is appropriate, and contributes to the clarity, style, and overall character of the story.	1 2 3 4 5

Ratings: 1 Poor 2 Fair 3 Average 4 Good 5 Excellent

What tools are available for digital storytelling creation?

A variety of different software applications are available that provide support for the creation of digital stories, and a number of examples are provided in the digital story creation section of the resources list. Some of these tools are expensive, and others are free. Purely online editing tools have become available as well as app-based tools for Android and iOS devices. The most notable computer-based tools are:

Microsoft Photo Story 3 is a Windows free download that allows for the manipulation of still images and audio using a wizard. It is an easy to use program most suited for young children but also usable with adults.

Windows Live Movie Maker is a Windows free download that allows for the manipulation of still images, video, and audio clips. The software application was previously built into Windows, but is now available separately, and is a more sophisticated application than Photo Story.

Apple iMovie allows for the manipulation of still images, video, and audio clips, and is preloaded with OS X.

Adobe Photoshop Elements is cross-platform compatible with Windows and OS X, allows for the easy modification of images and text slides, and is available in an academic version.

Goldwave is a digital audio editor that provides simple recording as well as more sophisticated processing, restoration, enhancement, and conversion for Windows and Linux. A free version is available for evaluation purposes, after which a lifetime license can be purchased.

In mobile contexts for tablets and smartphones, **WeVideo** is a useful tool for digital story creation. It is a web-based app, an Android-based app, and an iOS-based app. So, it is available across a wide variety of platforms and to many users. It is a free video editor that can mix images, text, video, and audio. Several free templates, with transitions, and corresponding images, effects and themes are available, while some enhanced functionality is only available in a paid upgrade.

How do I craft a digital story?

A four stage, step-by-step approach, to the creation of digital stories (based on Robin, 2008) is as follows:

Stage One – Define, collect, decide
- Select a topic for the digital story.
- Search for images (pictures, photographs, charts).
- Locate audio resources (music, speeches, interviews).
- Find informational content (PDF files, Microsoft Word files, Microsoft PowerPoint slides).
- Start thinking about the underlying purpose of the story, and aspects of narrative.

Stage Two – Select, import, create
- Select appropriate still and moving images for use in the story.
- Select appropriate audio as a background track or for sound effects.
- Select the content and text to utilize.
- Import images, video, and audio into the movie making application.
- Modify the number of images, or the image order, and clip audio/video where necessary.
-

Stage Three – Decide, write, record, finalize
- Decide on the underlying purpose and point of view of the story.
- Write a script to use for narration.
- Record the narration for use in the movie making application.
- Finalize by saving the digital story as a video file.

Stage Four – Demonstrate, evaluate, replicate
- Share the digital story with colleagues.
- Gather feedback on how best to further develop, expand, and implement the digital story in the classroom.
- Run a digital storytelling workshop.

In the TESOL context, however, a different approach is really needed as technology is not always required for these steps – nor is it always available. In this context, there are several steps to undertake when going about developing digital stories with students. Steps one through three can be done with or without a computer, tablet, or access to the use of technology, although steps four to six will, by their nature, require access. The steps that can be completed traditionally may be undertaken during class time with teacher support, or assigned for homework. So too, steps four through six, may be undertaken either in a technologically equipped classroom such as a computer lab, or by students at home if they possess the technological skills and equipment. Most importantly, these steps are a guide to understanding what is necessary for the process of digital storytelling development, and can be adapted for individual use.

Taking all of this into account, and in following the steps outlined by Jakes (2009), the production process might then, in TESOL contexts, follow steps that start with writing, script preparation, storyboarding development, then resource location and digital development prior to sharing.

Step One – Writing
Start students out with a topic or assignment where they will need to prepare no more than a 500 word narration.

Step Two – Script preparation

Work on tightening up the narration, and ensure that the maximum word count is not exceeded.

Step Three – Storyboarding development

To assist students in working collaboratively to lay out their ideas, a storyboarding handout, which may be found in Chapter 6 and photocopied for classroom use, can be provided: one that can be used by students when initially beginning to think about the development of their story, the media artifacts they might wish to include, and what they might wish their story to achieve or communicate. This provides a point from which students can then in turn begin to compose their narrative script, and space on the handout is provided for this purpose. Further, the storyboarding and scripting section of the resources list contains information on several applications that may be used with students when developing and constructing storyboards.

Step Four – Resource location

The next step would be locating the actual media resources that students require (images, music, sounds, and so on), and the resources list at the end of this book contains information on a number of means available for this purpose. This resource location step could be undertaken in the computer lab during class time, but it might prove better to set this task as homework. In a later lesson, students would then need to bring their media resources to the classroom on a USB stick, or access them through an online storage system (such as Dropbox, Google Drive, and so on).

Step Five – Digital development

The next step is that of actually creating the digital story, and this does require the use of a computer lab, or in-class use of tablets. Students would follow the storyboard that they had developed, and apply their media resources appropriately while using software to produce their digital story.

Step Six – Sharing

The final step then involves presentation of the created digital story. The presentation step can be conducted in class to a closed audience of teacher and students, or the digital stories could be shared privately online in a digital video archive such as YouTube.

To complete a digital storytelling activity in TESOL contexts, there are essentially technology-optional and technology-required steps. The technology-optional steps, one through three above, focus on a write, research, rewrite process, where narration leads to storyboarding. The remaining steps are the technology-required, where step four focuses on the location of media artifacts to accompany a developed narration, and steps five and six lead to the finalization, recording and ultimately the sharing of the digital story itself.

How would I use a tool to create a digital story?

There are many tools to choose from when deciding to make a digital story. One software-based tool is Photo Story 3, for which a free download is provided by the Microsoft Corporation, with the software working by stepping users through a wizard with each stage being completed in a set sequence. Regardless of the creation tool chosen, good preparation of images and audio (music and narration) is important. In the case of software such as Photo Story 3, or cross-platform options such as WeVideo, these digital story creation tools are very easy to use, especially for younger learners, and allow for the development of multimedia presentations that incorporate digital images, sound, narration, and various visual effects and transitions like zooming, scanning, and fading. However, Photo Story 3 does not process video, so the use of WeVideo or a more complex program such as iMovie or Movie Maker would be required for that purpose if required. So too, if seeking cross-platform flexibility, a web-based app such as WeVideo, which is also available as a native application for Android and iOS devices, would likely prove more suitable in the mobile context, or with older learners such as university students and adults.

A short overview in how to get started in using such tools follows, starting with Photo Story 3 and then moving to WeVideo. Please keep in mind that although tools do at times change the features that they offer, and at times the layout of the interface, or even may become defunct, the following guides have been written in a way that any such changes will not impact on understanding the essential mechanisms for using any of the digital story creation tools to develop a digital story project, and the ultimate publishing, saving, or uploading of it as a movie file.

Using Photo Story 3

Preparation

All digital images, sounds and narration files that students want to use in their project need to be collated and stored in a single directory on the computer. Storing all content in the same folder ensures that all project files can be easily found, and allows for easy perusal of potential digital story content by teachers and students before the movie making process begins.

Step One – Getting started

Open the Photo Story 3 software, and on the first screen select 'Begin a new story' and click 'Next'. You also have the choice here to edit a previously constructed story, or to play a story, from this initial start page.

Step Two – Importing and arranging images

Click 'Import pictures', then browse to the location where the digital story content files are located, and then select the images required to construct the digital story. Holding down the 'shift' key while selecting images will allow students to import a series of multiple files at one time, or a series of individual photos can be chosen by holding down the 'ctrl' key while selecting files to import. More images can be added at a later time by repeating this process. The software will import a wide variety of the most common image file formats (for example, BMP, JPG, PNG, TIF) up to a total of 300 images per movie.

After the selected images are imported, they will appear in the 'Timeline' view which allows students to select each image for editing or reordering. Images can be moved around the 'Timeline' by left-clicking on the image, keeping the mouse button held down, and dragging the image to a new position. Letting the mouse button go places the image in its new position. Images can also be selected one by one for simple editing like cropping and rotating, or by clicking the 'Edit' button to change the brightness, contrast, color, and so on. In addition, a number of effects can be applied to the photos including black and white, color pencil, and sepia. So too, clicking on the 'Remove black borders' option automatically ensures that all images are cropped to fill the screen. At this point, it is wise to click 'Save project' and save the Photo Story 3 project in the digital story folder that was created in the preparation stage. It is important to understand that all editing and saving during the project creation process does not alter the original files. To go to the next step, just click the 'Next' button.

Step Three – Customization:
Titles, effects, motion, transitions, and narration

Titles and texts can be added to any of the imported images by selecting the appropriate image and typing the text in the presented text box. The text can then be aligned to the top, center or bottom of the screen, and presented in various fonts, sizes, and colors. Simple effects can also be added to the images here by clicking 'Add effect', and they are the same as those outlined in the previous step. It might also be worthwhile to create a completely black image to use as a title or credits image at the start or end of the digital story, and it is useful for students to include information such as their names and student numbers in any digital submission. Click 'Next' to go to the following screen where narration can be added and the final files customized further.

In order to customize the movie further, select the image you wish to work with and click 'Customize motion'. You will then be presented with two versions of the selected image showing a 'Start' and 'End' position from which pans and zooms can be set by resizing the boxes that appear overlaid on the images. To zoom in, set the start image box to full size and reduce the size of the end image box. To zoom out, set the boxes in the opposite manner with full size on the end image and reduced on the start image. The duration for the image to appear in the movie can also be set here, but it is recommended that this be left as 'Set duration automatically' or, if it must be changed, be at least three seconds to a maximum of seven seconds. To review the changes just made, and to see if adjustments are required, click the 'Preview' button before clicking 'Save' to save the effect. It is helpful to set the start position to be the same as that of the previous picture so that any transition between images runs smoothly.

To incorporate transitions between images, click on the 'Transitions' tab located at the top of the screen. You will then be presented with the current image and the next image side-by-side with a preview of the transition effect between both of them. Select 'Start current picture using a transition', then choose the desired transition from the list of those available (such as 'Cross-fade'). Set the transition duration to automatic, and then preview the selection. After that, click 'Save' to save the transition before moving on to apply any other desired transitions to the remaining images. After all transitions have been applied click 'Close' to return to the narration editing screen.

To record a narration, first select the image you want to start recording sound over, then click the 'Record sound' button. Speak into the microphone to record the narration, then click the 'Stop' button to finalize recording. Press the 'Preview' button to see how the recording worked out, and if it is acceptable, you can move on; if not, you can repeat the process and record the narration once again. Narration can be recorded over one image at a time or over multiple images at one sitting. Either way, it is advisable to run the 'Sound hardware test' button from this page before attempting to record the first narration. This will ensure the microphone is correctly calibrated, and that the hardware and software are working well together.

Step Four – Background music

The next step is adding background music to the movie, and this can be done by clicking 'Select music' or 'Create music'. A number of music files can be added but it is important that the music be appropriate and preferably an instrumental version so as not to distract from the narration. If selecting 'Create music', you can use a selection of material presented by the Photo Story 3 software which includes the genre of music, the style of music, as well as the bands and moods of the music. The tempo and intensity of the music can also be adjusted, as well as the volume. After making the necessary choices, click on the 'Preview' button to hear how the music will sound. To have different music play over different images, just repeat the process while selecting the various images. After clicking 'OK', the background music then appears as a bar above the 'Timeline' and is automatically adjusted to end with the movie (even if you later decide to delete or add images). Then, click 'Preview' to see how the images and sound work together, and 'Save project' if the results are good or 'Delete music' to start over.

Keep in mind that your script, the recording of your narration, and your personal images belong to you, and that no matter what music you have chosen, even if you have composed it yourself, you should credit the source at the end of your digital story. Unfortunately, many companies today, like YouTube, will automatically block copyright material that you might want to use on a digital story, and this is regardless of the fair use copyright act. However, there are many sites offering copyright and royalty free music that can be used for digital storytelling projects – see the music resources section of the resources list.

Step Five – Publishing the movie file
In this final step, we convert the project file (or WP3 file) into a working movie file which can be exported from Photo Story 3 and saved in a format suitable for submission to the teacher, to send to friends and family, or viewed as part of a portfolio. In this step, a number of publishing options are available from 'Send the story as an email' to 'Save your story for playback on a smartphone', but with each option there is a trade-off in picture

quality and file size. Probably the best option to choose for the EFL or ESL teacher and student is the first one, 'Save your story for playback on your computer', then click the 'Browse' button to find the preparation folder (created earlier) as the save location. Follow this up by clicking 'Settings' to alter screen resolution settings if necessary (usually not required), before clicking 'Next'. Movie rendering will then begin, and this can be a lengthy process depending upon the number of images, text titles, and effects, the amount of motion, the length of time between images, the amount of narration, and the size of music files utilized in the project. After this process is complete, click on 'View your story'. The digital story is now complete.

Using WeVideo

Preparation

As with any digital storytelling project, particularly those involving EFL or ESL students, it is best to start out with a clear idea of what digital images, videos, sounds, and narrative script are going to be used to develop the project. This can be achieved by using the handouts at the back of this book, and by following the guidelines for working with students as presented in Chapter 10. Once the digital content and the narrative script has been prepared, WeVideo can be used to easily put together a short digital story using templates and themes, the drag and drop functionality, and with flexibility provided through cross-platform support across multiple devices from computers and tablets through to smartphones. The smartphone and tablet application, as well as the web interface version, have slightly different variations in capability and use, and it is up to the individual teacher as to which version affords the most flexibility and offers the most suitability to their teaching and learning context.

Step One – Getting started

If you are using an iPhone or iPad, you will first need to download the application from the App Store, or from Google Play if running an Android device. If using a computer, you should go to the WeVideo website. The digital story creation section of the resources list has more details regarding these applications and the website. If you are using the smartphone application, you can start to create videos immediately, and for free. These videos are saved locally to your phone, but they will contain a 'WeVideo' watermark in the top right corner, as well as an outro for a few seconds. The watermark is less obtrusive if using a tablet or smartphone for editing, compared to that placed onto videos when finalizing movies using the web interface. If using the website, you will need to first log into your account (or sign up for an account) which can be for personal, business, or educational use. From the web-based interface, projects are saved on the WeVideo server, and finalized movies can be published or saved to various locales such as Facebook, Google Drive, and YouTube.

Step Two – Importing and arranging content

After signing in to the website, you will be able to click 'Create new' in order to open the video editor and to start creating a video project. You also have the choice here to edit a previously constructed story if you have been working with the web-interface previously. However for those using smartphones, the application will launch straight into the video editor on opening. Smartphones have a large '+' button in the bottom right corner that allows you to select videos or photographs from the device. Tablets will offer a drag and drop interface that will allow you to drag media to the timeline, and this is similar to the website interface, which requires each photo or video to first be uploaded by clicking on 'Upload media'.

The photographs or videos can then be sorted into the correct order according to a previously established storyboard developed from a class handout or other in-class projects or homework assignments. Images and video clips can be moved around the 'Timeline' by left-clicking on the image or video clip, keeping the mouse button held down, and dragging to a new position. Letting the mouse button go places the image or video clip in its new position, and the length of time that each image or video is displayed can then be changed. On smartphones and tablets, this can be done by pressing to select the image or video and changing either the duration time of the image and its orientation (portrait or landscape), or by trimming the start or end of the selected video. On the website, each media artifact that has been imported can be individually selected and dragged to the required duration for images, or trim setting for videos.

Step Three – Customization:
Editing attributes, adding effects, motion, and titles

Once the order of images and videos, as well as their durations, has been set, you can start to think about customization. There are several methods of providing customization to a digital story when using WeVideo, and these include being able to add a theme as well as background music, both of which are discussed in the next step. In this step, the focus is on adding captions, animations (for example, scaling, positioning, fades), transformations (for example, rotation, flipping, fit), and effects (for example, sharpen, sepia, black and white).

Each image or video on the timeline can be selected with a click or a press, after which there are several options for customization. There is a 'Text' button on tablet smartphone devices that allows for captioning and text attribute changes, whereas the website offers an 'Edit' button to access this feature.

Captions can then be overlaid on the image or video, and the font, color, and other attributes (such as the duration of the captions being displayed) can then be altered. The image can be pinched to alter the scale and fit, or pressed and moved to alter positioning on tablets and smartphones. These options are also available through the web interface, but they need to be set individually by clicking on the 'Transform' tab, which appears next to the 'Caption' tab when editing an image or video. The 'Transform' tab is also next to an 'Animation' tab that allows for setting of image position (by placement and by scale, and by start and end point), as well as options for fading in and out. On tablets and smartphones, this option is available after pressing on the image for editing. Videos offer a 'Volume' tab across all interfaces, and this allows for control of the audio level of the clip which may need to be muted in order to allow for background music and narration to later become the focus. There is also a fade in and fade out option for each video clip that has been inserted on the timeline under the 'Volume' tab on the web interface, with the 'Transform' tab offering rotation, flip, fit, scale, and positioning options. A video 'Speed' control tab is also available through the web interface, if using a paid account, and this allows access to fast or slow motion control as well as editing tools such as Chroma key.

Finally, to add a title to the digital story, the first image can be selected and the title changed in a similar manner as adding a caption to an image. Text attributes (such as color, font size and type, and wording) can then be changed as desired. Otherwise, this image can be deleted and you can use an image or video of your choice with a caption overlay as a title. Alternatively, a theme can be selected to provide different start and ending options for the digital story, or one of several freely available backgrounds can be applied if using the web interface.

Step Four – Selecting themes, adding background music, overlaying narration

To work with various themes for a digital story, to add background music, and to overlay a narration, there are three buttons for these purposes. On the web and tablet interfaces, they are located to the left of the storyboard timeline; but on smartphones, they are located above the timeline which is represented vertically (instead of horizontally).

Selecting the 'Theme' button provides a series of free templates that each have their own unique introduction sequences, font formatting, and between image and video transitions for those using the web interface. The level of theme customization is slightly more limited when using the tablet or smartphone application as there are no transition options. Further, the tablet and smartphone interface offers only three free themes while the web interface offers substantially more. After selecting a theme, the web interface automatically inserts the themes transitions between the images and videos on the timeline. To change the type of transition, click on the image representing the transition between images and videos on the timeline. A number of choices from standard cross fades, flips, and wipes are available as well as various patterns like stars and diamond shapes, along with effects like curtains, paper planes, and flares to name a few. Also available through the web interface are various choices of backgrounds that can be used in place of images or videos in the timeline, with various effects and editing options available to customize these backgrounds, and they are similar to those available when working with images and videos. These backgrounds can also be used to end the video or start the video, and they can be used as an alternative to a theme-based ending or introduction sequence. Additionally available from the web interface is a simple text ending image that is similar to the standard text start image that is available across all interfaces. In any case, it is useful for students to include information such as their names and student numbers as a title on the initial theme screen, image, or background that is being used at the start of any project timeline.

Each theme comes with different background music, and this can be overridden by clicking on the 'Background music' button to the left of the timeline on tablet devices and for those using the web interface, or above the timeline on smartphones. Background music volume levels, particularly if using your own music over that applied by a theme, needs to be adjusted so that the narration can be clearly heard when the digital story is played back, and this can be done from the background music selection screen.

If you forego the use of a theme, and would like to simply add background music to your timeline project, WeVideo offers a very good selection and variety of background music from their freely available archive. The option of being able to select from a variety of freely available music that is licensed, so that your video can be made available in a variety of contexts, means that you can publish your finalized movie without copyright infringement issues. Alternatively, audio tracks of your own choice can be imported.

The final part of the project, and perhaps the most important one, particularly when engaging in TESOL, is providing the opportunity for students to speak, and in digital stories, this possibility comes in the form of narration. For digital stories, narrations are best prepared in advance so that they can easily be recorded and overlaid onto any intended digital story project timeline. For those using the web interface of WeVideo, there is a microphone button that once clicked gives the option to record the narration while previewing the recording and muting the audio. The narration must be recorded at one time, and in full, so this means a script must be well prepared in advance. Students can then click the 'Microphone' button to record their narration, and watch their movie play as they begin to speak. After recording is stopped, there is an option to adjust the volume of the narration before it is overlaid on the timeline. Those recording audio using their smartphone or tablet device are able to pause the recording as they go, whereas those using the web interface must record the entire narration at once. In either case, the narration can be erased or recorded over as many times as needed, but as previously stated, it must be made in a single recording session before it can be saved as an overlay to the timeline. Once students are happy with their narration, and it matches with the content of their images and video, the project side of digital storytelling creation is complete. All that is left now is to finalize the project as a movie file.

Step 5 – Publishing the movie file

Once all the images and video content have been arranged, and their attributes set accordingly, captions organized, the theme chosen, and any necessary transitions, title text, backgrounds, background music, and narration have been added to the digital storytelling project timeline, and students are happy with the result, the project can then be saved or published as a movie file. In the web interface there is a 'Finish' tab that once clicked, asks for a title for the video, and then provides a number of options for saving or publishing the movie. These options include setting the quality of the video, making the video private or public, and selecting one or multiple destinations. The destination options available via the web interface include: WeVideo, Vimeo, Google Drive, YouTube, Dropbox, Dailymotion, an ftp site, Box, and Facebook. Those using a tablet or smartphone are able to save the file locally, and are then able to send or publish to the location of their choice.

Although there is no time limit to the creation of movies using a tablet or smartphone, the free-to-use web interface does limit the exporting of videos to no more than two minutes per month. This time limit can be useful, as it forces students to be succinct, and to select their content and to word their narrations carefully. In this case, the time limit is displayed in the bottom right hand corner, and as the limit is per month, it allows the application to be used either for short courses or once per term or once per a semester. It should also be noted that digital stories can be created that are longer, but to finalize these as a movie an upgrade to a paid account would need to be secured.

What are the key points behind digital storytelling use in the TESOL context?

A number of key points emerge when considering employing the use of digital storytelling in the TESOL context:
Digital storytelling is a means for both teaching and practicing multimedia literacy.

- Digital storytelling can be tailored to effectively deliver specific content for learning.
- Success with digital storytelling comes solidly from being able to make meaning from experience.
- EFL and ESL students, working with images and text to create a digital story, develop digital literacy, media literacy, and visual literacy skills.
- Adhering to economy can prove to be one of the most difficult elements of the digital story developmental process.
- Evaluating the quality of student digital stories through a rubric allows for both ease of assessment of complex work, as well as assessing student output across a range of varied indicators across several categories of competency.

- A number of free, easy to use digital storytelling tools exist, and Photo Story 3 and WeVideo are two popular examples.
- The basic steps used to create a digital story are: define, collect, decide; select, import, create; decide, write, record, finalize.
- The digital storytelling production process, in TESOL contexts, consists of: writing, script preparation, storyboarding development, resource location, digital development, and then sharing.
- Digital storytelling does not require technology to complete all steps. In the traditional manner, there are classroom and homework tasks requiring completion prior to any technologically reliant tasks and this establishes a write, research, and rewrite process where narration leads to storyboarding. The location of media artifacts is then made to suit the narration before the finalization, recording, and sharing of the digital story.
- Digital storytelling resources abound, with the internet the best place to locate various resources.

Ultimately, digital storytelling provides a means for those professionals working within the TESOL field an avenue that allows learners under their care to begin to engage with multimedia in a way that provides students with a means to explore their own interests while customizing the learning process and content to their specific learning style, technological skills, and language learning level.

3. Multimedia Presentations: The Prezi Paradigm

3. Multimedia Presentations:
The Prezi Paradigm

Overview

Every student has, at some point in his or her academic life, been required to give a presentation, and in recent years, class presentations have needed to be tied increasingly to multimedia. It is here where Prezi offers a dynamic means of creating a multimedia-based presentation that can actively engage students, particularly in the smart board context where touch navigation is a key component, and one that allows for carrying out a variety of activities from within the same presentation. Prezi use also promotes active learning, with strengths of the presentation platform providing a unique way to establish interest in key topics, direct attention to various subjects, motivate and engage learners, and draw on the creative talents of students as they start to design and develop their own Prezis. The pedagogical possibilities arising from the use of the Prezi presentation paradigm in the context of teaching English to speakers of other languages (TESOL) are offered throughout this chapter, along with an overview of instructional strategies, tasks, and activities suitable for multimedia presentation development with learners.

What is Prezi?

With over 30 million presentations made daily (Swinford, 2006), Keynote is one system that people who prefer Apple applications may use, yet the more familiar and perhaps most ubiquitous presentation tool might be the Microsoft solution

PowerPoint. Both Keynote and PowerPoint are long standing presentation creation tools developed primarily for the business world, have been used for decades, and have a well-established classroom place and use. On the other hand, Prezi was initially developed by Adam Somlai-Fischer and released to the public in 2009 as a visualization tool with the aim of being intuitive to use, and to develop ideas and disseminate them in the form of a visual narrative that can transition from a big picture perspective to focus on specifics with ease (Lechlitner, Kocain, Reitz, Stroman, Kwon, Sheldon, Peedin, Chalfant, Robinson, Siebenhausen, Towns, Boldebuck, Applegate, Cain, & Cunningham, 2011).

Prezi uses a zoomable user interface (ZUI) that allows users to move around a canvas in both a linear and non-linear fashion. In other words, think of a Prezi as a large whiteboard that allows you to layout ideas, media, and connections, and move between the concepts these objects represent via non-linear transitions (Bruder, 2011). This allows for the emergence of creativity as presenters can essentially walk through a mind map, exploring and focusing upon the ideas emanating from each represented concept, while being free to move or zoom around non-sequentially between any place or part of these constructs (Crosby, 2010). This is in contrast to traditional applications like Keynote and PowerPoint that provide users with an avenue to develop slides that contain printable handouts, or showcase multimedia (audio, graphics, and video) in a single sequential file.

Prezi is available to teachers and students for free, and allows teachers to make Prezis either available publicly, make them private, or share them with select individuals. Public Prezis can be easily disseminated from the Prezi website; links to private Prezis must be emailed to others while other users can be invited to share the Prezi. Sharing a Prezi with others can allow for collaborative learning to occur, with students working in teams of up to ten people to edit the same presentation simultaneously, or to view the same presentation as a group while it is delivered by a presentation leader.

Prezi, like Keynote and PowerPoint, allows users to incorporate text, graphics, audio, video, and other presentation objects such as PDF documents and YouTube videos. Prezi presentations are primarily created and stored online, but they can be downloaded for local presentation. A desktop application is also available by subscription that allows for local development of content where offline construction may prove necessary.

How can I use Prezi?

Prezi offers a dynamic means of presentation that can actively engage students, particularly in the smart board context where touch navigation is a key component in technology use. The Prezi workspace allows for development of contextual relationships between objects at a glance, which helps to engage students visually. The non-linear pathway format allows information to be provided in a flow, which engages students mentally by going with the normal thinking process. Grouping, layering, and zooming promote a focus to engage students in a discussion that can in turn promote deeper understanding of content presented.

In the view of Laurillard, Stratfold, Luckin, Plowman & Taylor (2000, p. 2), multimedia environments allow for learner control over navigational pathways with narrative lines only established "from an interactive collaboration between the user and the program". This means that educators need to be aware that learners engaged with learning from Prezi content may come to perceive the presentation as something very different to the expectations of the presenter if they do not follow a presenter established navigational pathway, or if one is not provided for them to follow before engaging in their own exploration of a Prezi as a concept map, particularly since, computer-based instructional variance can be explained by the unique navigational selection of students (Schar, Schluep, & Schierz, 2000).

Nonetheless, the workspace element of Prezi, being a large and flat canvas, allows students to lay out the different elements of their presentation in any arrangement that they desire. These elements can then be tied together by a navigational pathway that allows users to move backwards and forwards around each element in a linear progression if they want to. This kind of canvas layout is great for any student, adult or child, who needs to brainstorm, move elements around, figure out an order, move things again, and maintain flexibility over the final outline of their actual presentation (Leimbach, 2010). Students are limited in the amount of text that they can type into text boxes, but this can ensure that their ideas are succinct and are more point- then paragraph-oriented. The formatting of backgrounds and choices with color are also limited to only a few, but this in turn sees students focus more on content objects and how these relate to each other over the actual look of their presentation.

As for teachers, the grouping, layering, and zooming functions allow for key points or features to be hidden in the dot of the 'i' or 'j', and in the period at the end of a sentence. Even tiny explanations, definitions or translations can be associated with keywords in the passage, and zoomed in upon as assistance is required. This function can also be applied to images by the use of frames to zoom in to an area of a graphic – asking students predictive type questions, for example – then zoom out to show the entire image. Details of larger images that are easily lost can also be focused upon in this manner. So too, PDF documents or videos can be embedded in presentations to provide examples, or to further offer clarification of points, but videos have been limited to 50 MB in the free version.

What type of educational Prezi can be made?

At the elementary school level, Prezi can be used to assist with story sequencing, solar system layout and labeling, or in developing water and plant life cycle storybooks. In secondary education, Prezi can be used to illustrate themes from literature such as *To Kill a Mockingbird* or to present an historical event from World War II. In computer classes, the preparation and comparison of PowerPoint and Prezi application and development can occur. In post-secondary education, students may create a timeline on Prezi based on a novel in a communications class, provide steps in food preparation in culinary arts, or develop a virtual playbook for use by a coach in sports (Lechlitner et al., 2011). Pinto Pires (2010) also highlights a number of educational uses for Prezi which include displaying a biography-based timeline by creating paths from dates to life event descriptions, by zooming from place to place on a map during geography lessons to provide details and facts about areas, and displaying historical information of a place or person by date and then zooming into the associated facts and details so that they can be reviewed.

What elements are behind an effective Prezi?

The key to creating an effective Prezi is in the development of grouping and layering of objects and concepts.

1. Deal with one concept at a time, and cluster content that is connected contextually.
2. Use images over text, as they can represent the essence of the idea that you are trying to convey and are visible when zoomed out.
3. Let your voice be the text of the Prezi, either live while presenting, or by a recorded narration.

Clark (2011) also reminds us to consider the entire canvas as conveying meaning, and suggests using the canvas to create concept maps. He also mentions wrapping the Prezi around a story or metaphor to provide a creative framework to assist students in internalizing concepts. Another suggestion is to provide increased interactivity to engage students in the presentation by integrating participatory activities, such as Poll Everywhere, so that students can provide their own input into an ongoing presentation.

Remember that the point of a presentation is to provide clear communication of information. Outline the Prezi presentation beforehand (perhaps using some other mind map software, or even type up an outline in point form in a word processor), and of course stay in control. Keep the content and size of the Prezi manageable in terms of presentation length, grouping, layering, and navigation choices. Ultimately, to give a flawless presentation, practice the presentation somewhere else beforehand and keep an offline backup for contingency purposes.

How can a Prezi lend itself to TESOL?

Educators working in countries where a visual learning style predominates can use Prezi to great effect in the English as a foreign language (EFL) context. The tool can also be used to establish interest in key topics, direct attention to various subjects, motivate and engage learners, and draw on the creative talent of students as they start designing and developing their own Prezis. Students can develop skills associated with mind map development, demonstrate their linguistic level, and reinforce their learning while practicing the language skills that they have already fostered to date.

Prezi has also been used to improve student vocabulary in the secondary school EFL context (Aljehani, 2015), and is recognized by Robinson (2014), along with Peridore and Lines (2011), as the kind of tool that provides learner engagement in the English language arts (ELA) and EFL classrooms by bringing written lectures to life.

However, in and of itself, Prezi will not improve student learning. It requires strategic employment of Prezi to create opportunities for active learning, and to capitalize on the strengths of the presentation platform to engage students in the learning process. Further, as Prezi provides a platform for incorporating a variety of different kinds of multimedia file types, each 'slide' can be multimodal and allow students to demonstrate their understanding and knowledge of learning content in their own unique way, fitting with multiple intelligence and multiple ways of learning (Rhinehart Neas, 2012).

How can I start using the Prezi presentation paradigm with students?

As Prezi enables educators with the ability to provide students with a presentation, it can be used in the TESOL classroom just as any other presentation software is used. The Prezi focus can be teacher-centered, student-centered, or a mix of both depending on the use of the editor and on the aim of the lesson being taught. The benefit of Prezi use is that it can contain all the needed components and resources required of a single lesson in one presentation.

In a teacher-centered process, Prezi can be used to enrich existing text-based (or even other internet-based) material, from practice tasks through to language games. A number of traditional EFL classroom activities can also easily transfer to the Prezi setting. For example: teaching new ideas and concepts at the start of a chapter or topic, reviewing vocabulary through practice and drill tasks or quizzes, and providing review material.

In a student-centered process, Prezi work on a topic can be undertaken individually or collaboratively. During the collaboration process, students' speaking and listening skills can improve during concept development and design discussions, while their reading and writing skills can improve during presentation construction. Students can design presentations on any topic from food to fashion. These presentations can be assigned to individuals or as collaborative group work, with each individually created or group created Prezi later coming together as a part of a larger class Prezi. In this manner, each group or individual student would be responsible for completing a single node, or concept, that would come to form part of a larger class Prezi presentation which can be given in class or be archived for later topic review.

Other uses of Prezi in the EFL classroom may include teaching phonics, grammar, vocabulary, writing, and storytelling. Students could also use the tool to complete comparison and retelling tasks, and develop poster projects. Sabio (2010) provides a range of Prezis for teacher reuse, from writing (such as introductory paragraphs, types of sentences, descriptive writing) to speaking (for example, phrasal verbs, relative clauses, quantifiers).

Meanwhile, Prezi for Education is the Prezi educational community home, and offers discounts to educators upgrading from their free account. Also available is the Prezi Education Blog, where posts showcase the use of Prezi in the education context.

How do I evaluate a Prezi?

Prezi presentations can be evaluated just like any other (including those provided by Keynote or PowerPoint) through the use of prefabricated rubrics like the example to soon follow. In this case, several overall constructs are being assessed that include:
- presentation of the problem being discussed,
- the background information provided,
- the design and content of the presentation itself,
- resolution of the problem presented, and
- actual oral presentation skills.

As always, rubrics should be provided to learners beforehand so that they understand what will actually be assessed, and ask questions if they don't understand.

Although it is useful for the busy teacher to apply pre-made rubrics, it is even better if teachers formulate ones of their own which can reflect their teaching environment and the points they wish to assess. One good source for this is Rubistar, where there are a number of premade evaluation options as well as information on how to create unique context-sensitive evaluation instruments. The rubrics section of the resources list also contains several other rubric creation tools that may prove worthwhile to look over.

The rating scale used in the following rubric goes from 1 to 5, with 1 being poor, 2 fair, 3 average, 4 good, and 5 excellent. 'Average' is used as a midpoint so that students can see how each particular skill relates to peers. This allows teachers to identify those skills that are weak in individual students, and those that may need improvement.

Assessment Item	Assessment Criteria	Score
Problem Introduction	Sufficient information is provided, and presented clearly.	1 2 3 4 5
Background Information	Sufficient information is provided, and relevant.	1 2 3 4 5
Content and Design	Too much or too little information per slide; animations, colors, font size, and sounds are appropriate.	1 2 3 4 5
Problem Resolution	Logical progression of argument with facts supporting the solution.	1 2 3 4 5
Oral Presentation Skills	Speakers clearly understand the content, and aim the presentation at the audience (in terms of vocabulary use, rate of speech, and so on).	1 2 3 4 5

Ratings: 1 Poor 2 Fair 3 Average 4 Good 5 Excellent

How do I get started with Prezi development?

Although the blank canvas and non-linear presentation style of a Prezi can be empowering, it can also be debilitating for first time users, including students, who may need a lot of guidance in getting started. Further dangers include creating mega-maps that house an overwhelming amount of data, and going overboard with zoom transitions (or jump cuts) from topic to topic, which leads to panning that can cause a form of motion sickness amongst the audience (Leberecht, 2009). Working with a Prezi involves being able to develop a concept map, or mind map, of your project as well as working with a canvas and moving from a big picture view of elements down and through a more detailed and layered structural representation of ideas. This may prove quite challenging for students if they approach Prezi creation in the way they would create a linear Keynote or PowerPoint slide.

Potter (2011) has established several guidelines to assist with initial Prezi development, and a few of these are:

Structure first, detail later

Outline your presentation, determine what the big picture top-down view of the canvas will look like and make this draw in viewer attention, while simultaneously serving to function in support of the presentation subject matter.

Make group sections large

The Prezi canvas is essentially unlimited in size, and everything is zoomed in to fill the presentation frame as required. This means that you can lay out objects over a wide area, with no need to later cram everything in next to each other or have to waste time moving lots of objects around just to fit one more in.

Select themes early

Choose a theme that best suits your presentation and stick with it from the start. This is so that fonts on titles and text in parts of the Prezi presentation will be uniform, and will always stay where you position them and what you position them within.

Avoid transition overuse

Move progressively and consistently between items rather than wildly oscillating around the canvas, zooming in here, out there, and in again somewhere else. Remember, even though the presentation medium may provide you with lots of eye candy, only use additions to your presentation that add value to the content that you present. For example, Prezi can go really big and really small and this can be used to advantage by zooming in on something that a user may not guess is there from the initial top-down view.

Use a uniform style

After establishing the sizes that you want for titles and text in various sections of your Prezi, use the duplicate and edit functions to ensure that all other titles and text are of the same sizes and fonts. Keep in mind that every image used will fill the presentation window, so they must be large and crisp in their native sizes. By the same token, use frames to advantage by setting an invisible frame around groups of objects or small images, as it is the frame that takes the focus and comes to fill the presentation window when Prezi zooms in on it. Also, rely on the quick keys when working with Prezi; for example, holding shift functions to move groups of objects at one time while keeping their spatial relationship intact. Finally, either embed a YouTube video so that it will automatically play or, alternatively, add the video URL as free text and click on it to play it only as required.

How do I work with a zoomable user interface?

The key to understanding and working with a zoomable user interface (ZUI) is to completely comprehend the relationship between the conceptual objects that you are placing on the Prezi workspace or canvas and the ways in which these ideas will be linked both hierarchically (in terms of magnification layers) as well by group (in terms of providing a navigational pathway between and among each object and group). To begin with, blocks of content need to be arranged contextually in relation to each other, as users will zoom from one block to another, and down within these blocks to see more detailed views at different levels of magnification. Each block of content can hold several layers of magnification, and this means that a user can zoom into one block from a big picture view showing several blocks, then zoom into an image within the magnified block (filling the presentation frame), and then zoom further down into that image to another object such as piece of text (a YouTube video, a PDF document, or simply a more specific detail of the original image), whose view once again comes to fill the entire presentation frame. The opportunity that these presentation options provide, as Watrall (2009) describes, goes beyond presenting content as chunks strung together in a linear fashion. They provide access to content in a more logically related manner by presenting sets and subsets that are connected spatially and can be navigated non-linearly as well as linearly.

How would I create and house a Prezi?

The Prezi website offers very simple and detailed getting-started tutorials which are all very succinct and comprehensive. If you choose to get started straight away, the directions below can help you gain a brief overview of Prezi development before signing up and creating your own account.

Step One – Write

In a Prezi, the entire canvas is the presentation workspace. To get started, simply double-click anywhere on the canvas, and a text box will appear where you can type in a key idea. Ideas can be placed anywhere and dragged around the canvas if more space is required. The canvas is essentially an infinite workspace.

Step Two – Zoom

After adding text-based ideas to the canvas, the zoom feature of Prezi can be used to focus on each of these ideas and allow you to add more text to develop them further. Additional text can be placed anywhere on the canvas at any zoom magnification level. Magnifier buttons are available from the right side menu, or the mouse wheel can be used to zoom in and out of the Prezi.

Step Three – Border menus and text boxes

After clicking on a text box, a menu appears, and it can be used to control several attributes of the object that you have clicked on. The various menus at the top and to the left and right of the Prezi canvas will allow you to arrange all of the text ideas, and establish levels of hierarchy through manipulation of size and placement on the canvas.

Step Four – Importing images

Adding images to the Prezi is controlled from the top menu. Simply click 'Insert' and then 'Image' to locate a local file for import, and after an image appears on the canvas, click on it to activate a menu that controls the placement, size, or other attributes of the image as desired. Prezi development will be faster and smoother if all the images that you wish to use for the Prezi are already collated in a single folder.

Step Five – Develop a presentation narrative

Once all the text and images (along with other files that you may want to use, such as PDF documents or YouTube videos) are arranged in your Prezi, a navigation pathway or a view path can then be chosen. Use the magnifier buttons or mouse wheel to zoom out to look at the entire canvas, as viewing the 'big picture' can assist in establishing the right view path for the Prezi. Click on 'Edit path', then develop your navigational pathway by clicking on each object in the order that you want them to be shown. The order can be changed at any time by dragging an unassigned path ball (the one that appears between path numbers) onto an object, or by dragging a path number away from an object to a blank space on the canvas. It is often a good idea to start out with some meaningful imagery that can be traced or woven through when finalizing the view path.

Step Six – Present and share the Prezi

Clicking on 'Present' moves the Prezi into presentation mode. You can then step forward or backward through the Prezi using the arrow buttons or keyboard arrow keys. In 'Show' mode, you can zoom in or out from each object or you can freely move around the canvas, and a click on the arrow button will return the presentation to the preset navigational pathway. If desired, you can click the 'Share' icon to invite others to view or edit the Prezi, or to obtain an embed code for use with a blog, Moodle, or other web page. The Prezi can also be shared to social media, or it can be downloaded as a PDF document or as a portable Prezi under this icon. The presentation itself will always be housed under your account on the Prezi website, and it will be accessible to you from any web browser.

To assist in getting started with students, a number of photocopiable handouts, including a practice exercise and tutorial, are available in Chapter 6.

What are the key points behind Prezi use in the TESOL context?

A number of points to bear in mind while deploying Prezi with students are:

- Prezi uses a zoomable user interface (ZUI) that presents sets and subsets of information that is connected spatially, and can be navigated both non-linearly as well as linearly.
- The Prezi workspace allows for development of contextual relationships between objects at a glance, helping to engage students visually.
- The non-linear pathway format of Prezi presentations allows information to be provided in a flow that engages students mentally by going with the normal thinking process.
- Grouping, layering, and zooming promote a focus to engage students in a discussion which can in turn promote deeper understanding of the relationships that exist amongst the content being presented.
- Students following their own narrative line to explore a Prezi as a concept map may perceive the presentation as something very different to the expectations of the presenter, and this needs to be kept in mind when students use Prezi presentations on their own for learning.
- While sharing and working collaboratively on Prezi development, students' speaking and listening skills can improve during concept development and design

discussions, while their reading and writing skills can improve during presentation construction.

- Working with a ZUI requires a good comprehension of the relationship between conceptual objects placed on the workspace and the ways that these will be linked both hierarchically as well as by group.
- Stay in control. Keep the size and content of the Prezi manageable in terms of presentation length, grouping, layering, transition use, and navigation choices.

Software applications like Keynote and PowerPoint may still have their place in the classroom today, but Prezi affords educators and learners an alternative presentation platform. Such a tool offers a dynamic means of presentation, and presentation collaboration, that can engage learners and keep their focus in ever increasing visually oriented touch-driven teaching and technology environments.

4. Supporting Instruction: Podcasting and Screencasting

4. Supporting Instruction: Podcasting and Screencasting

Overview

Podcasts and screencasts are both disruptive innovations in that they started out using existing technology in ways that were different from intended practice (Christenson & Raynor, 2003), and they create a new market and value network that has since led to 'significant societal impact' (Assink, 2006). In the classroom, podcasts and screencasts can also be viewed as potentially disruptive by expanding the notion of audience from that of an audience of one (the teacher) or a few (classroom peers) to that of many (potentially the entire population of the globe). Further, by employing multimodal ways of knowing to expand the analytical and critical insights of learners (Hadjioannoou & Hutchinson, 2014), the use of podcasts and screencasts for learning holds the potential for the authentic use of content in ways that allow for the transmediation of knowledge that occurs in ways that are very different to those prior to the beginning of the 21st century, and in ways that allow students to become producers rather than consumers of knowledge-based media products.

Ultimately, this chapter focuses on the use and applicability of podcasts and screencasts in the context of teaching English to speakers of other languages (TESOL), and the means of supporting and supplementing instruction with podcasts and screencasts is detailed. Attention is placed on the types and effectiveness of podcasting and screencasting with learners, along with an overview of instructional strategies, tasks, and activities suitable for episode development with second-language learners of English. The steps involved in planning, producing, and publishing episodes are also presented. This is all reinforced with a variety of useful resources to assist students and teachers in starting out with podcasting and screencasting.

What are podcasts and screencasts?

In contrast to the mass produced broadcasting of content to a general audience, both podcasts and screencasts can be described as the narrowcasting of content, with authors providing specific knowledge, information, and insights to members. Narrowcasting in the classroom might see peers produce content for each other as well as interested stakeholders (like parents, the administration, and the teacher), which in turn allows them to become producers rather than consumers of media. In addition, as podcasts and screencasts not only allow users to selectively choose content, or subscribe to individual providers, this allows for the sustained exposure to specific content or knowledge over time, along with the ability to time- and place-shift access to this content, leading to anywhere, anytime listening or viewing – knowledge-on-demand.

Knowledge-on-demand (KOD), as Sampson, Karagiannidis, Schenone, and Cardinali (2002) see it, has emerged from the needs of a knowledge-based society that requires access to the anyone, anytime, anywhere delivery of education and training that is "adapted to the specific requirements and preferences of each individual citizen". Daily (2007) also suggests that, for technologies like podcasting and screencasting, there is the promotion of just-in-time (JIT) learning over just-in-case (JIC) learning. It is also likely that both access to content that individuals were specifically interested in, along with information that they needed 'right now', has led to the popularity and normalization of podcasting and screencasting with wider and wider audiences in a relatively short space of time.

Podcasting defined

The term *podcast* is one of several suggested by Hammersley (2004) for 'portable on demand' listening. Today, podcasting is usually recorded in the MP3 audio file format, but it can also be video-based (for example, appearing in the MP4 file format), and it can be played back on a variety of devices from smartphones to computers. Each new episode can be downloaded automatically (being either pushed or pulled) to a podcatcher (aggregators) capable of reading feed formats such as Really Simple Syndication (RSS), and are formats distinguishable from other digital audio or video formats like streaming media. Once the file has been listened to or watched, it can be automatically or manually deleted when another episode is to be released into the *podosphere* by the *podcaster* (the author or producer of a podcast). Normally, subscriptions to a podcast are free, and as such, there is essentially no cost for listening to or joining, and becoming a member of, a feed.

Terminology that has been used in association with podcasting and screencasting includes, among many more, terms such as: *vodcasting, vidcasting,* and *vlogging* for video podcasts; *blogcasting* for the podcasting of blog content; *Godcasting* for the podcasting of religious content; and, *learncasting* for the podcasting of educational content.

Screencasting defined

The term *screencast* was proposed by both McDonald and Cooley and chosen by Udell (2004) to represent the emerging genre. Screencasts capture what you do on any device with a screen (for example, a computer or an interactive whiteboard).

Think of a screencast as a movie, where the stage is the display, the content the star, and you are the narrator. In many ways, screencasts can be thought of as video podcasts, and are mostly recorded, edited, and then published inside a web page or a blog post, or uploaded to a learning management system (LMS) like Moodle, Edmodo, or Schoology (as opposed to being distributed automatically by a feed). Screencasts are also often uploaded to public video sharing sites like YouTube where viewers might subscribe to the screencasters channel. Like podcasts, screencasts can humanize e-learning and enhance the educational experience of learners as they combine audio, text, and video, so that lessons can become more engaging and at the same time more accessible to a wider variety of learners – especially those that may need aural and visual explanation of content being presented to them simultaneously.

How can I use podcasts and screencasts?

Perhaps the best way to use podcasts and screencasts is in providing support for and supplementing direct instruction, which can take learning outside the classroom and also provides students with a means of creating their own learning content. Bell, Cockburn, Wingkvist, and Green (2007) have identified a number of positives and negatives associated with podcasting in educational contexts, some of which include access, flexibility and appeal. Simultaneously, these technologies can provide a fresh approach to engage students and improve the revision and instruction process while harnessing the promise of multimedia to enhance student learning (Mayer, 2003; Davis & McGrail, 2009; Liou & Peng, 2009).

Podcasts and screencasts provide flexibility as they allow students to listen to, or watch, an archive of course related content that is available anytime anywhere, and allows for flexible learning and convenience of access while being engaged in other activities or multitasking. This however could mean that student attention is not focused on the learning material as environmental factors could impact upon concentration and the ability to hear content effectively, or occur in environments that may prevent note-taking (for example, public transport). Podcasts can also be appealing to those students who prefer auditory-based learning, and to those who do not like to read or may have problems with reading (for example, dyslexia). By the same token, screencasts might also appeal to those students who do not have reading problems but prefer aurally and visually oriented learning materials.

Podcasts and screencasts can also be useful for those learners who might have missed a lecture if the class is recorded, as it can provide a first listening and note-taking session. The recording can also be used to gain access to a second listening by those who might need it (for example, second language learners). Such material can also be used in exam preparation as well as for reference purposes, and it allows students to review and study the content at their own pace, facilitating self-paced learning and perhaps also aspects of learner autonomy (Holec, 1987). Misuse might arise here though, as students might only use the podcasts and screencasts to review for exams or in cramming sessions rather than rely on other study methods.

Nevertheless, both podcasting and screencasting provide the opportunity to encourage active learning, and different types of learning, from visual (including videos, infographics, PDF content, resource links, and so on) through to aural (listening clips). They can also involve students kinesthetically if the students themselves are engaged in the process of development of a podcast or screencast, and are involved in the preparation of any associated materials to use with it. The production process of both podcasts and screencasts is also well suited to provide for the development of multiple skills (for example, reading, writing, listening, and speaking) as well as multiple literacies (including that of digital and media literacies).

What types of podcasts and screencasts exits?

Almost anything can be turned into a topic for a podcast or screencast. As such, there is a great number of different podcasts and screencasts available, from the educational to the simply entertainment-based genre. Overall, however, there are only four main distinguishable types of podcast and four main distinguishable types of screencast, with different forms of content suited to one type or another.

Podcasts
Solo
Generally presented as a monolog, the solo podcast is one person talking on a particular topic where content can include news, opinions, or tutorials. It may be the easiest podcast to create as it involves only one person, and a script. The challenge here is to retain audience interest with just one person speaking.

Interview
An interview format can be added to a solo podcast as a feature episode, or be established as the regular type of format from the very first episode. The challenge is to maintain a stream of interesting guests, as well as ensuring adequate recording quality (particularly if the interview is done over the phone or low-speed internet).

Multi-host

The multi-host type of podcast has more than one person talking or hosting the episode. This can allow for a more informal tone than a solo podcast, provide more than one viewpoint on a topic, spread the production effort, and allow for a show to continue if a presenter is absent. The challenge here may be the need to pay particular attention to scheduling as there are more people involved in planning and producing the podcast, and this may also lead to higher editing needs.

Video

A *vodcast*, *vidcast*, or a *vlog*, is the same as a podcast but with video. It can provide an interesting and engaging format for a podcast, particularly one that is presented solo. However, challenges here are the editing needs from using video as well as audio, the need for higher-end production equipment, and ensuring a 'studio' that is quiet and free of audience distractions or annoyances (for example, those that might appear in the background).

Screencasts

Presentation

Presentation screencasts are usually lectures that are delivered while recording the presentation slides of a particular topic along with the narration of the speaker as voice-over. Challenges here can involve the editing out of pauses as well as issues concerning the updating of slides or other information at a later stage.

Demonstration

In this type of screencast, the screen is usually recorded to illustrate how to use a particular application or how to navigate a particular website. The screen is recorded with voice-over as narration. Challenges here are the need to keep talking and telling the user exactly where to look and what they need to do for each step. A script is essential with and editing to include annotations, captions, callouts, and zoom effects.

Streaming

A streaming screencast is played 'live', as it happens, but can be recorded simultaneously for later editing and archival purposes. Challenges here are ensuring that the bandwidth that is available to viewers allows for high resolution transmission of data, particularly if there is a reliance on visuals that the audience must interpret or be able to read. Further, the equipment being used must be reliable, so that there is no break in the transmission, and powerful enough to record the screencast without interference to the live stream.

Whiteboarding

The whiteboarding screencast captures the activity displayed on interactive whiteboards, from applications being used on various devices in a similar fashion, or from any blank canvas (such as a white slide in a presentation program) that is being used to simulate a whiteboard canvas. The challenge here is to write legibly so that the content is easily readable. Typically, the whiteboard is being recorded while the author provides a voice-over to accompany the visuals. The challenges here include ensuring that the handwriting is legible, and that the narration is audible. Also editing, depending on the application used to capture the activity, may not be possible, so attention to detail and correctness becomes imperative.

What elements are behind an effective podcast and screencast?

An effective podcast or screencast consists of several essential elements, and among the many points that can be discussed here,the more important involve preparation, structure, focus, highlighting of key points, editing, feedback, and scheduling. The effectiveness of each of these attributes will now be discussed for both podcasts and screencasts.

Podcasting

Preparation

Make notes before the show, and follow them. Do not attempt to improvise during the episode. Prepare questions for guests ahead of time, and provide these to guests prior to the episode recording. The notes and questions can then be used as the introduction, and as a reminder piece for show notes. Ensure that your hardware is of a good quality, and that it is functioning properly to avoid annoyances and problems during the recording.

Structure

Structure the podcast with a beginning, middle, and end, and use musical or sound collages to transition between topics. Title your podcast in a compelling way, and to reflect the content of the show. Keep the show length suitable to the audience: twenty to thirty minutes, up to an hour, or even as a little as five minutes.

Focus

Keep topics brief, and limit the coverage of each topic to between three to eight minutes.

Highlighting of key points

Use guests to vary the pace and tone of the episodes, but always bring them back on track if they go off topic. Get into a habit of repeating their key points for members for reinforcement. Remind members that you are documenting the key points, and that they will be included in show notes along with any resources mentioned regarding these points.

Editing

Delivery doesn't have to be perfect – use a human voice – but remove long pauses and significantly large errors from the episode. If something is funny laugh about it 'on air', but edit your laughter if it goes on for too long. Collate any resources or anything else that was mentioned to include in episode notes, and send a copy to the guest. (They may provide corrections or a few more 'nuggets' of information to include). Prepare the notes and the RSS feed and, when scheduled, release the episode and the accompanying show notes.

Feedback

Invite conversation by asking listeners to discuss the podcast. Take on board constructive feedback, and adapt your podcast accordingly. Ask for topics that listeners might want to hear about, initiate competitions, and involve members in the show.

Scheduling

Make it regular (for example, once a week). People who subscribe rely on you to release your podcasts on time! Episode 'air dates' need to be consistent, with a new episode released every week or every few weeks on a schedule that is both doable for you and familiar to subscribers. It is also important to update listeners if there will be a delay in the upload of a new episode. Perhaps prepare a podcast that can be used as a filler episode if something does happen to prevent your scheduled episode from being released on time.

Screencasting
Preparation

To create a script and notes that will guide the screencast, start with an outline and then perform a walkthrough before you begin recording. When recording, it would be a good idea to follow these notes and to make no attempt to improvise except to include a comment here and there, especially to mention a point that you think is important but forgot to include on the initial walkthrough. Ensure that your hardware is of good quality and is functioning well to avoid annoyances or problems during recording. For example, automatic updates are turned off along with notifications to prevent them from popping up during recording.

Structure

Briefly introduce the topic, and provide a brief layout of the information to be covered (for example, how there are ten steps involved, and that there will be the use of two applications to achieve this). Have all of your 'screens' or areas to be recorded set up and sized appropriately, especially if you intend to move between applications or from one to another in a set sequence. You can use different applications, tabs in a browser, still images, or perhaps even a view of yourself over a webcam to create different screen areas. Ensure that the screen areas for capturing are all the same size, and break the screencast into sections by using these screen areas at the appropriate times.

Focus

If you need to go off topic, or provide a detailed explanation for something, prepare an image that can be shown on screen. Alternatively, you could switch to record yourself on webcam, in which case you need to look presentable. This technique will get members familiar to either seeing you or the same image when more specific information is being covered. In either case, try to focus on audience needs. Also, pause as required, take a break so that you can remain focused, and stay on top of things while recording.

Highlighting of key points

Tell the viewer what they should be looking at, and use the mouse to highlight specific areas where viewers should be looking. Overlay annotations, captions, and callouts, and zoom into screen areas as necessary. Depending on the software being used, this can be done on the fly but it will likely have to be performed during the editing stage.

Editing

Remove comments that do not add anything to the screencast, like, "Oh, look. *My alarm on the calendar just went off. Now let me see here. … Oh, okay. Right, then. Yes. … Let me go ahead and close that app then. …"* (The app should have been closed prior to recording). If any edits like this are made they should be edited out. Also, review your screencast for continuity issues, and ensure that your narration and video are synced. Record your video and narration at different times if necessary, or rely on software that records these as different tracks to make the editing process easier. When recording, be careful of exposing confidential data (like passwords). These will need to be removed during editing, or covered in post-production, if they do appear on screen. Add any overlays to add value to your cast (annotations, callouts, captions, zooms, and other effects like transitions or music).

Feedback

Invite comments – ask subscribers to provide feedback on the screencast, and to leave comments on your channel. Take on board constructive feedback from viewers, and adapt your screencasting technique if necessary (for example, if you are talking too quickly). Reply to comments if viewers ask for clarification of something presented on screen, or for further information about something that you have mentioned in the screencast. You may need to add an additional element to the screencast if there is a consistent issue among members. Ask for topics that subscribers want to see screencasted, and attempt to involve subscribers in the show (for example, by addressing comments online by selecting a few to highlight and a few to respond to at the end of the following screencast).

Scheduling

Casts need to be regular, released every few weeks or once a month, and on a timetable that becomes familiar to subscribers. In that way, viewers are likely to be eager to watch your next episode as soon as it is uploaded to your channel. The content that you choose to screencast will determine how long it will take to produce, and this will need to be considered when creating release schedules and 'air dates'. It is also important to update your channel members if there will be a delay in the upload of a screencast, and it may be a good idea to develop a screencast that can be used as a filler episode if something does happen to prevent your scheduled episode being released.

How can podcasting and screencasting lend themselves to TESOL?

Podcasting and screencasting can assist in the development of several language skills (such as speaking, listening, and pronunciation) during the production and narration stages of creation, as well as reading, writing and vocabulary development during the preparation stages. Students who participate in the production of podcasts and screencasts can also become familiar with the development of various forms of communication techniques (like, interview, speech, and presentation skills). Both formats will lead students to engage in listening skills practice, as well as seeing them concentrate on the need to speak effectively with attention to speed, pronunciation, and clarity of voice. Multiple literacies (from traditional literacy through to digital literacy and media literacy), along with other essential skills that include research skills, time management skills, and problem-solving skills, can also be developed through student podcast and screencast production and use.

Teachers too can also use podcasts and screencasts both directly and indirectly for teaching and learning. They can be used as supplementary content in a course to provide news and updates, answer student questions, and review content. More innovative uses include the provision of formative and more personalized feedback to students, and the reworking and resequencing of content (Ali, 2016).

A number of traditional TESOL classroom activities can be easily transferred to the podcast or screencast setting. These might include, but by no means limited to, activities involving commentaries, interviews, presentations, speeches, storytelling, retelling, and review. Additional activities can also include: developing a walking tour of a school or campus, recording a 'talk show', engaging in sportscasting, demonstrating the use of an application, or critiquing peer-developed podcasts and screencasts.

Teachers can use podcasts and screencasts to create targeted resources that are reusable, are used to resequence classroom or textbook content, and can be used both in and out of class for better use of the available time. An example is the development of language-point review podcasts, where students go over phrases or specialized vocabulary that need to be learned as part of a course (like idioms or aviation terminology). Another example might see screencasts being used to present new vocabulary, using an audio- or video-based flash card method with one student saying the word and the other giving the definition, and trading off on this procedure as they record. A further example is flipping the classroom, where content is first introduced and learned through a podcast or screencast for homework, with time in class spent on practice and review.

Podcasts and screencasts can also be used by teachers to cover content that is necessary, but these are more suitable for review outside of class time (for example, grammar points, or functions of language), leaving the classroom free for speaking and other more targeted activities. Students themselves could also be tasked with creating podcasts and screencasts that go over such points as well as essential vocabulary, and even be responsible for summarizing classroom content for later examination review and for peers who have missed a class. Screencasting students can annotate their work as they show it on screen, and, depending on the software used for editing, include interactive quizzes for completion. In either case, students who are responsible for developing podcasts and screencasts can begin to take control of the learning process, and this can lead to higher motivation. It also allows them to produce content that can then form part of a digital portfolio, and material that can then be assessed based on student performance – rather than continually provided work that is teacher-delivered.

Teachers may wish to record parts or the whole of their classroom activities as a live screencast or podcast over the course of a year or term, and they will have material that is reusable and ready to archive after editing. In this way, teachers who are taxed for time can still begin to develop content with minimal production time involved. However, those teachers that do have more time could specifically record mini-lectures, or short 'show-and-tells' to present the main points covered by each class or unit, and provide a personalized example of the format of work expected to be produced by students. An example of this for a speech class sees the teacher write a small speech using the model available to students from their textbooks, but personalizing it with content from their own life when conducting the screencast. In this manner, the teacher will have students engaged with content on a very different level from any text or any accompanying publisher video. This kind of podcast or screencast not only provides additional material for review, but it provides an increased connection to the teacher along with development of multimodal learning. For distance learners, or those engaged in blended or online learning, establishing a personal connection with the teacher through just such content can be important for continued study success.

Further, teachers when providing feedback or advice on student submissions can use podcasts and screencasts. In conversation, or in speaking classes, teachers can note any student errors and mistakes made throughout the week, and provide examples of usage in a mini-podcast that can be assigned for out-of-class listening each week. It is podcasts like these that could also be retasked for use as in-class activities, with work sheets and additional tasks set in conjunction. In writing classes on the other hand, students can submit work digitally and, rather than using tools that track changes when editing these submissions, teachers could use a screencast to provide personalized descriptive feedback. This kind of feedback is made by recording the screen and verbalizing any explanations, corrections, comments, and annotations made to students work, while simultaneously highlighting any points of note (both excellent and poor) as you go. All of this can be conducted in what would normally be set aside as grading time anyway. This particular kind of screencast could be applied to virtually any kind of digitally submitted work (like essays, infographics, and slideshows), and provides a way to add a more personalized touch and an additional means of establishing a connection with students over that usually obtained via rubrics or comments written on assignments.

How can I start using podcasts and screencasts with students?

There are a great number of sources from where to begin looking for podcasts and screencasts to use in the classroom. When accessing these sources it might also be helpful to look at content from one of three different perspectives: traditional, expert, and classroom.

Traditional content
Traditional content can be provided to students as audio or video recorded material for students to use to catch up if they have missed lessons, or for students to use as a review of any classroom introduced content. Examples might include providing resource links to TOEFL test podcasts or screencasts, or links to podcasts and screencasts that cover the kind of

grammar points or language focus introduced by the weekly topic or unit.

Expert content

Expert content can easily be retasked or used directly as supplementary material for homework or alongside textbook content, and this can be in the form of amateurs interviewing experts or the experts themselves talking or presenting on a particular topic. If teaching English for specific purposes (ESP), or general English to medical majors at college level, this might include finding podcasts and screencasts on health topics where specialist doctors are interviewed on the topic areas that are also touched on by the class textbooks.

Classroom content

Classroom content is where students and the teachers themselves would begin to produce their own material as podcasts and screencasts which would see students beginning to share specific insights into their learning, critique completed tasks, activities, or peer work, and engage in a variety of production techniques that could potentially lead to language practice and linguistic development. Examples could then be shared to the internet and redistributed to all learners in the form of a podcast or screencast.

Accessing sources

A variety of podcasts and screencasts are readily available for incorporation into the classroom, and to be used as a means to augment lesson content. These include those focusing on elements such as: English for specific purposes (like business English and medical English); current affairs topics; grammar topics; idioms; slang; songs; vocabulary; and much more. Sources for gaining access to a range of podcasts and screencasts on different topics and genres like these, aside from conducting a search on iTunes or Google, include the following:

ESLPod provides a range of podcast content tailored to second-language learners of English, from specific topics through to test taking guides.

Podcast Alley is the place to go if you want to find out the latest news about podcasts, and to gain access to the top podcasts.

QT-ESL Podcasts provides a range of podcasts, covering oral grammar practice, and which include scripts and worksheets.

TED Talks provide talks of various lengths in a presentation video format that is given by experts.

YouTube provides a great deal of user-generated content, and also a large number of screencasts and the opportunity to subscribe to channels.

Accessing content

In order to begin using podcasts and screencasts with learners, students will need to know how to download or subscribe to them, how to listen to them or how to view them, and how to gain access to any podcast show notes or screencast program notes that are available. In most cases, you as the teacher will be able to provide the necessary web links to the content that you require your students to view or hear, but if you are using a particular podcast or screencast channel consistently, then you may need to show your students how to subscribe to the appropriate content provider. If you want them to develop their own podcasts and screencasts, you will certainly need to provide materials and tutorials to teach them how to plan and produce this kind of content (perhaps by developing a podcast or screencast yourself) as well as developing or gaining access to a rubric to evaluate final products.

How do evaluate podcasts and screencasts?

Perhaps the most appropriate means available to evaluate a podcast or a screencast, particularly in the TESOL context, is to use a prefabricated rubric based upon a Likert-type rating scale. Any such rubric should be presented to students beforehand, so that they can understand what will be expected of them and what will be assessed.

Evaluation rubrics, particularly those using indicators across several categories, are essential when assessing the quality of student work on any complex multimedia-based project. Although it is useful for the busy teacher to apply pre-made rubrics, it is better if teachers formulate their own that reflect their teaching environment and the points that they wish to assess. One good source for this is Rubistar, where there are a number of pre-made evaluation options as well as information on how to create unique context sensitive evaluation instruments. The rubrics section of the resources list also contains several other rubric creation tools that may prove worthwhile to look over.

Here are three sample rubrics that can be used with students in any classroom, including those participating in podcast or screencast production from within the TESOL setting. The first focuses on podcasts in terms of student planning, production, and publishing, the second focuses on the planning, production, and publishing of a screencast, while the third looks at providing a means for assessing the quality of student produced scripts or narrations intended for use in the production stage of a podcast or screencast.

The rating scale used in the following rubrics go from 1 to 5, with 1 being poor, 2 fair, 3 average, 4 good, and 5 excellent. 'Average' is used as a midpoint so that students can see how each particular skill relates to peers. This allows teachers to identify the skills that are weak in individual students, and those that can be improved.

Podcasts – Student developed

Assessment Item	Assessment Criteria	Score
Introduction	Tells the audience who the podcaster is, the date and location, and what to expect.	1 2 3 4 5
Content	Clear purpose, and a constant focus placed on presenting the topic to the audience.	1 2 3 4 5
Delivery	The show flows well with a conversational tone maintained; volume of the voice is constant.	1 2 3 4 5
Language	Specialized vocabulary and grammar are used correctly; definitions provided.	1 2 3 4 5
Conclusion	Clearly summarizes key points, directs listener towards show notes, and invites participation.	1 2 3 4 5
Technical	The podcast is of a good length, transitions are well-timed, sound levels are consistent, and everything is audible.	1 2 3 4 5
Show Notes	All resources mentioned are included, and access to the notes is easily available.	1 2 3 4 5
Group Work	All people in the group had a role, and participated equally toward the finished product.	1 2 3 4 5

Ratings: 1 Poor 2 Fair 3 Average 4 Good 5 Excellent

Screencasts – Student developed

Assessment Item	Assessment Criteria	Score
Introduction	Topic overview provided, and expectations set.	1 2 3 4 5
Content	Clear purpose, and a constant focus placed on presenting the explanation to the audience.	1 2 3 4 5
Delivery	Screencast flows well, with a conversational tone maintained.	1 2 3 4 5
Language	Specialized vocabulary and grammar are used correctly; definitions are provided.	1 2 3 4 5
Conclusion	Clearly summarizes key points, directs listeners towards program notes, and invites subscriber participation.	1 2 3 4 5
Technical	Transitions are smooth; sound levels are consistent; everything is audible. Annotations, callouts, captions, and zooms are appropriate, and add value.	1 2 3 4 5
Program Notes (if included)	All additional resources or links mentioned are included, and access to notes is available.	1 2 3 4 5
Group Work	All people in the group had a role, and participated equally toward the finished product.	1 2 3 4 5

Ratings: 1 Poor 2 Fair 3 Average 4 Good 5 Excellent

Podcasts and Screencasts – Script/Narration

Assessment Item	Assessment Criteria	Score
Introduction	Provides relevant information.	1 2 3 4 5
	Establishes a clear purpose, and states the objectives of the podcast/screencast.	1 2 3 4 5
	Engages with the audience.	1 2 3 4 5
Content	Creative and original content that enhances the topic(s).	1 2 3 4 5
	Well-researched, with all information accurate and informative.	1 2 3 4 5
	The direction of the show (podcast topics or screencast explanations) follows a logical sequence.	1 2 3 4 5
Podcasts only	Well-edited 'questions' for experts or guests, with potential for follow-up.	1 2 3 4 5
Screencasts only	Well-edited 'quotes' from experts, credited appropriately.	1 2 3 4 5
Language	Vocabulary enhances content, grammar is used correctly.	1 2 3 4 5
Show/Program Notes	Resource links are all functional, and appropriate.	1 2 3 4 5
	Everything is cited, or credited correctly if not copyright free.	1 2 3 4 5

Ratings: 1 Poor 2 Fair 3 Average 4 Good 5 Excellent

What tools are available for podcast and screencast production?

There are a number of commercial and free applications available to create podcasts and screencasts, and more examples are provided in the podcasting, interactive whiteboard, and screencasting sections of the resources list. Some of these tools are expensive, while others are free. Purely online editing tools have become available as well as app-based tools for Android and IOS devices. Here are some of the most notable.

Audacity is a free multi-track audio recorder and editor that contains some very powerful features, including those for adding effects to files and conducting analysis of the audio recorded. It is one of the most popular tools for podcasting.

Garage Band is available for Apple products, and can be used to create audio-only and enhanced podcasts.

Pod-O-Matic allows for the upload of audio and video files, from either a computer or from a media library on another device, for hosting on their servers.

FeedForAll allows for the creation, editing, and publishing of RSS feeds.

Feedity is an online tool to create an RSS feed for any webpage, and there is an option to upgrade to a premium account that offers additional features.

FetchRSS: RSS Generator is an online RSS feed generator that can create a feed out of almost any webpage, automatically update the RSS feed when new content is added to the page, and generate an RSS feed for a social networking site.

Screenchomp allows users to annotate pictures or to use the application as a whiteboard. Any work completed with the application can be saved automatically to the internet.

Screencast-O-Matic offers 15 minutes of install-free branded recording time for the free version, or 60 minutes recording time for the branding-free paid version. Any screencast created can be saved locally to their server, or to YouTube.

TechSmith Camtasia Studio is one of the most comprehensive screencasting editing tools available, and provides a great deal of control over the creation process. It also has a great range of extensive features including a large number of transitions, zoom effects, and noise reduction capabilities. Files can be saved in a variety of formats both locally and to the internet (for example, screencast.com and YouTube). It has a higher learning curve than other tools have, and although it is on the more expensive side for many educators, it is one of the most popular and comprehensive screencasting tools on the market.

How do I plan and produce a podcast or a screencast?
Planning a podcast or screencast

Once the tools to create and distribute a podcast or screencast have been selected, the pre-production, production, and post-production aspects of development can be considered. To this end, the following steps will assist.

Podcasting
A potential model to follow when planning out the development of a podcast is as follows: planning → producing → publishing → promoting.

Planning

Starting out podcasting, either as a teacher or getting students to create their own, is best done by creating one that is shorter (say, five minutes) rather than longer. Whatever the length, developing a podcast involves the need for planning to meet the intent of the broadcast. There needs to be an outline, if only to determine if there needs to be one long episode or a series of shorter episodes. The style of the recording (audio or video) needs to be chosen, along with a quite location to maximize the recording quality.

Producing

For this component of podcast creation, the hardware and software needs to be obtained. At a minimum there needs to be a suitable computer, microphone, and audio recording software. A web camera or screencasting software will also be required for a video podcast.

Publishing

The podcast will need to be uploaded to a hosting service, and an RSS feed created to distribute the episode. Show notes and links to various resources discussed in the podcast will need to be hosted on a site or made available for download.

Promoting

An effective means to promote the podcast is to get listeners and guests to suggest future topics, ask questions, suggest other guests to interview, and take part in contests. In addition, links to the podcast feed and show notes, and behind-the-scene photos, can be spread across various social media sites like Facebook and Twitter.

Screencasting

Potential steps to follow when considering the development of a screencast are: topic → objectives → format → scripting→ capturing → editing → publishing → promoting.

Topic

Select the unit or lesson that will be covered.

Objectives

Determine the learning objectives based on the selected unit or lesson.

Format

Determine the screencast format based on the unit or lesson covered, and in light of the lesson objectives (for example, demonstration, presentation, tutorial).

Scripting

Walk through the steps on screen that you intend to discuss in the screencast, type out a script as you go, and read through the script before beginning any recording to determine the timing. Keep both the needs of the viewer in mind and the prepared objectives in mind, and keep language to that of an everyday conversational tone.

Capturing

Decide on the area of the screen that will be recorded. Any narration or script can either be recorded live or added in post-production so that it matches with on-screen activity, but this will depend on the software being used. Callouts and zooming, along with various other effects, can also be added when editing, but they do need to be considered at this stage. Keep on topic, don't get distracted, and don't be afraid to pause the recording to rest or take a sip of water if needed. Speak clearly and slow enough for viewers to be able to follow along easily.

Editing

After recording the screencast, a variety of media can be edited in enhance the recording from the narration itself through to additional animations, music, photos, and video clips. Other features such as zooming or callouts to grab attention and orient the focus can also be added. Less is more – edit to capture only what the viewer needs to see and leave the rest on the 'cutting room floor'.

Publishing

After finalizing the editing process the screencast can be saved as a movie file or uploaded to a YouTube channel or a learning management system (LMS), or it can be distributed for in-class delivery.

Promoting

The audience of your screencast will depend on how you promote it, and a class blog or class website will ensure that various stakeholders will also be able to gain access to any developed content once the screencast is published. Screencasts can also become evidence of classroom activities and form part of a portfolio for both the teacher and the students.

Producing a podcast or screencast

There are several steps that are unique to podcast and screencast production – no matter what hardware or software is being used to record them, and no matter where associated links and show notes will be hosted, the feed used for any distribution, or any social media sites used for promotion. The length of both podcasts and screencasts should be based on the selected topic, interest, or points under review or presentation, but they need to maintain continuity whatever their length, with the minimum being five to six minutes (for example, when reviewing a point or discussing a shorter topic). They can be for an hour or more (for example, when a class is recorded, a tutorial provided, or a specialist is interviewed). Here are some example production steps, with associated timings and comments on the process involved.

Podcasting production steps
Introductory music (30-60 seconds)
Play a unique identifier for your show that audience members can associate with you. This can then lead into the podcast, with the introduction monolog as a voice-over.

Introductory monologue (30-60 seconds)
State who you are, introduce any guests, and state the topics to be discussed.

Topics (3-5 minutes each)
Stay focused on the key aspects of the topic by asking guests a specific question (or posing questions to yourself), and guiding guests back on track where necessary. It is advisable to prepare a script for solo podcasts. Throughout each topic, remind the listener that any resources or links will be posted as show notes, and where these can be obtained.

Closing remarks (2 minutes)
Thank the audience for listening, thank any guests, mention the topic and/or guests of the next show, and remind the audience where to go for show notes.

Closing music (2 minutes)

Play out the podcast with the same music tack as used in the introduction. This can be started during the closing remarks and continue afterwards.

Screencasting production steps

Introduction (30-60 seconds)

Select the screen area that will become the focus, and provide a voice-over introduction to the topic or topics that will be discussed, with an overview of the steps involved.

Topics (3-5 minutes each)

Each topic-based section needs to stay on script, keep the viewer informed, and tell them everything that you are doing. Zoom into and highlight features only when they are being discussed, use annotations and callouts where necessary, and edit out any pauses or mistakes in post-production.

Closing remarks (2 minutes)

Finish off by thanking the viewers, and reminding them of the topics covered, the knowledge and skills that have been imparted by watching the screencast, and how these skills can now be put to use.

How would I use a tool to produce and publish a podcast and a screencast?

To begin podcasting or screencasting, several technological tools are necessary. Typically for podcasts, typically a device capable of running audio recording software and possessing a built-in microphone would be the minimum required. For screencasting, access to a device capable of running screen recording software and recording audio, and that has a built-in web camera, is the minimum. Software that has the ability to highlight the mouse location, create zoom effects, and create on-screen annotations (like callouts and text), along with an external microphone, should be considered. Places to publish the final product need also be taken into account. For podcasts this might involve the development of RSS feeds and a place to host transcripts and show notes such as a blogging site, while screencasts may be uploaded to a YouTube channel with program notes and a transcript posted in the description. To assist in developing a transcript to include, along with show and program notes, voice recognition software would be required. To begin either podcasting or screencasting, you will need the hardware, the software, the time, and the topic. Rather than focusing on providing a tutorial for the use of each software item required, the focus here will be placed more on the steps involved when going about publishing and promoting a podcast or screencast.

Preparation

To produce a studio-quality podcast, you will need access to several resources:

- A device capable of recording and saving your episodes.
- An external microphone, along with a pop filter or pop shield, is strongly recommended, although a built-in microphone could be used.
- An application to record your voice and to save the file for editing and file conversation.
- A voice-recognition application to convert your audio file to written text, or to perform the conversion in real-time, so that subscribers will be able to access a transcript of the podcast.
- A text editing application to edit the transcript, and show notes.
- An image editing application to create your cover art.

- A site to host your podcast file, transcript, images, and show notes.
- An application to create an RSS feed of your podcast.
- A plan to publish and promote your RSS feed across multiple platforms.

Step One – Content development

The first step in creating a podcast is to plan it out, and then produce it, and the steps involved in this process have already been outlined. You should also be familiar with any copyright issues that may impact your broadcast. Once you have recorded your MP3 or MP4 file, then you can begin to edit it, trimming silences, and any mistakes or periods of awkwardness.

Step Two – Transcription

To start to convert a podcast episode into a transcript, the use of voice-recognition software like Dragon Naturally Speaking would be ideal, but for a short podcast, it could be done manually. The transcript should be saved in PDF file format, and no matter how it is generated, be sure to read through the transcript to ensure that it is correct and error free. You will then need to tidy it up so that it reflects your podcast appropriately, and this includes adding pertinent information to the file such as the podcast title, air date, images, most certainly identifying who is saying what and when, and when each section starts (like, identifying each new topic discussed).

Step Three – Show notes

One you have a transcript you will be able to search through it for keywords, so that you can begin to generate links to all the resources, applications, products, and whatever else was mentioned in the show. If you have identified all of the items to be included in show notes with an audible tag (like the phrase 'show notes') as you recorded your podcast, then this will be a relatively easy task to perform. The show notes should contain all the appropriate details associated with the podcast episode (for example, title, air dates, and images) to identify your podcast.

Step Four – Cover art

You will need to create a JPG or PNG file to use as the cover art, or a podcast album cover, of your podcast. The image file should be a minimum of 1400 x 1400 pixels and a maximum of 3000 x 3000 pixels, and it should also be clear when scaled down to a size of 50 x 50 pixels. You might decide to use a photograph and overlay the name of the podcast on the photo, but remember that this image will become representative of your podcast to all of your subscribers. If interested, a number of example images can be seen on the cover art of the podcasts found at the podgallery website. At this point, you should also perform a search to confirm that the name of your podcast is unique before you begin to find a hosting provider.

Step Five – Hosting

After you have all of your podcast files complete, you will then need to find a place to host or store them (the audio/video podcast file itself, the transcript, the show notes, associated images, and so on). A number of places exist for free hosting, including blogging sites like WordPress.

Step Six – Posting and tagging

WordPress has built in support for podcasts while a number of other platforms do not. It is advisable to create a new page with a new domain to be used as your feed, and WordPress allows for a number of domains and sites to be included under the one username. To create a podcast post after creating your site, generate a normal blog post and tag it with the keyword 'podcast'. After that, use the WYSIWYG (What you see is what you get) editor to add all your podcast files and to create the content, look, and the hyperlinks that will point to all your podcast episode files. It is this URL that will be used to create the RSS feed.

Step Seven – Feeding the podcast

To publish a podcast to iTunes or other places so that people can search and subscribe to it, you will need an RSS feed, and you can create this with a number of sites, from FeedBurner through to FETCHRSS: RSS Generator. For now, to use FETCHRSS: RSS Generator, or simply FetchRSS, you will need to register. A free service is provided which allows for a feed limit of five, is updated daily, and shows the last five updates with text-based ads. The free service would be sufficient for many teachers, as the feeds are deleted if no one is reading them after seven days, but it also has a paid service. It should be noted that you can use any web page to create a feed.

Step Eight – Creating the feed

To create your first feed automatically, go to the FetchRSS website, enter the URL of the webpage you would like to convert into a feed, and then click 'Continue'. You will then be taken to some subscription options, of which the free plan would be the most suitable to select at this time. After that, you will be able to click 'Go to my RSS list' where you will be able to see each feed or link that you have converted into an RSS feed. You will also be able to download the RSS feeds as outline processor markup language (OPML). The OPML file is useful as it can hold all your RSS subscription information for backup and sharing. Although not required, you could also use an application called Feedly to import your OMPL file, or use the online application OPML Viewer to view the contents of the file. The code of each feed can also be read by clicking on the name of the feed.

Step Nine – Configuring the feed

From the 'My RSS list' page, you will have several configuration options that include 'Settings' from where you can change your login data, and 'Plan' from where you can select a paid subscription as well as options for configuring, disabling, deleting, or reading your feed with any aggregator. You also have the option to access a 'manual RSS builder' if you would like to go that route. Click on 'Config' to change the details associated with a feed, such as the title, description, and the number of news items in the feed. Click on 'Disable' to disable the feed, 'Enable' to enable it at a later time, and select one of the other options to get the feed in other formats, including Atom (an XML syndication format), CSV (for use with spreadsheet programs), or JSON (Java Script Object Notation). If you no longer want to keep the feed, click 'Delete' to remove it from the list.

Step Ten – Publishing and promoting the feed

One of the most popular vehicles for podcast distribution and discovery is iTunes, and there are other options including Google Play Music (depending on geographical location) and places like SoundCloud. To submit your RSS feed to iTunes, you will need to go to 'iTunes connect', sign in with an Apple ID, and provide your RSS feed for validation. If approved, your podcast will be listed in the iTunes directory, but if not, you can still use your RSS feed on any of your PDF files (including the transcript and the show notes), and promote your podcast across a range of other platforms (for example, Facebook, your blog, and your email signature). Clicking on the feed would open a listener's favorite news aggregator into which they would be able to download and listen to all (yes, all) of your podcasts. You should also provide this information as a 'Call to action' at the close of your podcast, telling your listeners how and where to subscribe so they can automatically receive any future podcasts that you produce.

Screencasts

Preparation

To produce a high-end screencast you will need access to several resources:

- A device capable of running screen recording software and of recording audio.
- An external microphone with a pop filter or pop shield is strongly recommended, although a built-in microphone could be used.
- A web camera, if you wish to record yourself as you provide a voiceover.
- An application capable of recording on-screen applications as well as audio.
- An application to edit your recording and capable of highlighting the mouse location and creating zoom effects and on-screen annotations such as callouts and text is highly recommended.
- A voice recognition application to convert the audio of your recording to written text, or to perform the conversion in real-time, so that subscribers will be able to access a transcript of the screencast.
- A text editing application to edit the transcript and program notes.
- An image editing application to create your channel art.
- A site to host your screencast channel, where you will upload your files, transcripts, and program notes, and from where your viewers can subscribe.
- A plan to promote your screencasts and channels across multiple platforms.

Step One – Content development

The first step in creating a webcast is to plan it out, and then produce it. The ways to do this have already been outlined, and you should also be familiar with any copyright issues that may impact your broadcast. Once you have recorded your MP4 file, then you can add additional items of focus, such as annotations, callouts, and zoom effects, and edit out any silences, mistakes, or periods of awkwardness.

Step Two – Transcription

To start to convert a screencast into a transcript, the use of voice recognition software like Dragon Naturally Speaking would be ideal, otherwise for a shorter screencast, it could be done manually. The emerging transcript should then be saved in PDF file format, but be sure to read through the transcript to ensure that it is correct and error free. You will then need to tidy it up so that it reflects your screencast appropriately. This would include adding pertinent information to the file such as the screencast title, air date, images, and when each section starts (for example, new topics and applications being discussed) starts.

Step Three – Program notes

One you have a transcript, you will be able to search through it for keywords so that you can generate links to all the resources, applications, products, and the other things that are mentioned in the screencast. If you have identified all of the items to be included in program notes with an audible tag (like 'program notes') as you recorded your screencast, then this will be relatively easy. The program notes should contain all of the appropriate details associated with the screencast episode (for example, the title and air dates), along with any associated images that identify your screencast.

Step Four – Channel art

Although channel art is not necessarily required, it is a good idea to use it as an identifier for your screencasts (perhaps at the beginning and end of all your episodes). In this case, you would need to create an image file with dimensions of 2560 x 1440 pixels, and no larger than 4 MB. You may decide to use a photograph, and overlay the name of the screencast on the photo. Remember that this image will become representative of your screencast to all of your subscribers.

Step Five – Hosting

After you have all of your screencast files complete, you will then need to find a place to host or store them (like the screencast video file itself, the transcript, the program notes, and associated images). A number of places exist for hosting video files including YouTube, TechSmith Screencast.com, and Vimeo where you can also include hyperlinks to external files hosted on sites such as WordPress, and provide a link back to your screencast.

Step Six – Channeling screencasts

On YouTube, you can create a channel with a unique name for your screencast, and link this to a Google+ page of the same name. This allows for management from a single account. The upload and conversion process of videos may take some time, after which you will be able to edit them from the 'Video manager'. Links added to the 'About' page of your channel will also be featured below your channel description, and they can include one to your website, one to your podcast, and others to social media like Facebook, Twitter, or Instagram.

Step Seven – Channel video editing

Once your screencast is hosted or uploaded onto YouTube, you will be able to see it from the 'Video manager'. Clicking on the 'Edit' button to the right of each video that you have uploaded provides you with a variety of editing options that include: general information and settings (including titles and descriptions), enhancements (such as stabilization, filters, and blurring of faces), audio (where you can choose ad-free tracks as background music), annotations (where you can overlay text on the video), cards (which can be used to overlay clickable hyperlinks on the video), and subtitles (where you can upload your transcription for use as this feature).

Step Eight – Carding, annotating, and subtitling channel videos

Perhaps the most important features on offer for a TESOL screencaster relying on YouTube as a channel provider are the 'Annotation', 'Card' and 'Subtitle' features of the 'Video manager'.

The 'Annotation' tab allows you to add a 'Title', 'Notes', and 'Speech bubbles', and to 'Label' or 'Spotlight' an area. All of these, aside from the 'Title' allow you to also add a hyperlink to a 'Video', a 'Playlist', a 'Channel', a 'Crowdfunding project', and most importantly to 'Subscription' where you can help people subscribe to your channel or to others.

The 'Card' tab also provides a series of overlay options that include the ability to add an information card to promote a 'Video or playlist', promote another 'Channel', 'Link' to an external website, or involve subscribers by encouraging them to participate in a multiple-choice 'Poll'. The poll feature can be used to ask review questions of students as the video progresses, and these questions can tie with any worksheets for later classes or for post-viewing. Additional annotations can be added to suit different classes that might require links to different content from the same material, or are learning different points from the same content. This allows for reusability of any created screencast with different levels of language learners.

Finally, the 'Subtitle' tab will allow you to import your transcript and sync it with your video. This feature can be turned off and on, and may prove useful depending on the level of second-language learner that you are teaching. It is also a useful feature that will allow learners to continue watching your screencasts if they do not have headphones, and are in public places (such as a library) where they will need to mute their device.

Step Nine – Feeding the screencast

To further promote your screencasts, you can, as with a podcast, rely on an RSS feed, and you can create this with a number of sites from FeedBurner through to FETCHRSS: RSS Generator. For now, using FETCHRSS: RSS Generator, or simply FetchRSS, you will need to register. A free service is provided which allows for a feed limit of five, is updated daily, and shows the last five updates with text-based ads. The free service would be sufficient for many teachers as the feeds are deleted if no one is reading them after seven days, but there is also a paid service. It should be noted that you can use any URL or webpage to create a feed.

Step Ten – Creating the feed

To create your first feed automatically, go to the FetchRSS website, and enter the URL of the webpage that you would like to convert into a feed, then click 'Continue'. You will then be taken to some subscription options, and the free plan would be the most suitable to select at this time. When you click 'Go to my RSS list', you can then see each feed or link that you have converted into an RSS feed. You will also be able to download the RSS feeds as outline processor markup language (OPML).

The OPML file is useful as it can hold all your RSS subscription information for backup and sharing. Although not required, you could also use an application that imports your OPML file, or use the online application OPML Viewer to view the contents of the file. The code of each feed can also be read by clicking on the name of the feed.

Step Eleven – Configuring the feed

From the 'My RSS list' page, you have several configuration options that include 'Settings' (from where you can change your login data), and 'Plan' (from where you can select a paid subscription), as well as options for configuring, disabling, deleting, or reading your feed on FeedHub (an online News Aggregator). You also have the option to access the 'Manual RSS builder' if you would like to go that route. Click on 'Config' to change the details associated with a feed such as the title, description, and the number of news items in the feed. Click on 'Disable' to disable the feed, 'Enable' to enable it at a later time, and select one of the other options to get the feed in other formats, including Atom (an XML syndication format), CSV (for use with spreadsheet programs), or JSON (Java Script Object Notation). If you no longer want to keep the feed, click 'Delete' to remove it from the list.

Step Twelve – Publishing and promoting the feed and channel

One of the most popular vehicles for podcast distribution and discovery is iTunes, and along with places like YouTube, it can also be used to host your screencasting content. To submit your RSS feed to iTunes, you will need to go to 'iTunes connect' and sign in with an Apple ID, and after that, you will be able to provide your RSS feed for validation. If approved, your screencast will be listed in the iTunes directory, but if not, you can still use your RSS feed on any of your PDF files (including the transcript and the program notes), and promote your screencast across a range of other platforms (for example, Facebook, your blog, and your email signature). Clicking on the feed would open a listener's favorite news aggregator into which they would be able to download and watch *all* of your screencasts. You should also provide this information as a 'Call to action' at the close of your screencast, and by telling your viewer to click on the 'Subscribe' button to your channel if hosting your screencasts on YouTube.

What are the key points behind podcast and screencast use in the TESOL context?

A variety of key points associated with podcasts and screencasts that are important to keep in mind when using the technology with language learners include the following:

- Podcasting and screencasting offer new ways to provide traditional learning content through the transmediation of content, and offer innovative and creative ways to perform traditional tasks.
- Podcasts and screencasts allow for the narrowcasting of content, and for time- and place-shifting of its consumption.
- Podcasts can prove appealing to students who prefer auditory-based learning, and to those who do not like to read or may have problems with reading. Screencasts may appeal to those same students, as well as those who prefer aurally and visually oriented learning material.
- Both podcasting and screencasting provide the opportunity to encourage active and targeted learning.
- Teacher-produced episodes should be kept short and on point, focusing on learner needs, particularly if flipping the lesson. Clarification can be undertaken in class.

- A number of sources are available for podcast and download subscription as well as applications for their development. The type of content that can be produced can stem from traditional material (textbooks and the set curriculum), the expert (a guest lecturer), and the classroom (student generated content).
- Engaging students in episode production leads to listening skills practice, concentration on speaking with attention to speed, pronunciation, and clarity of voice in particular.
- Planning a podcast or screencast requires listening and discussion while collaborating, as well as reading and writing while constructing the production plan itself.
- Multiple literacies, along with other essential skills (for example, research, time-management, and problem-solving) can be developed through episode production and subscription.
- The four main types of podcast are solo, interview, multi-host, and video. The four main types of screencast are: presentation, demonstration, streaming, and whiteboarding.
- Thoughtful and careful editing, along with thorough planning, are key to good development. Keeping on topic, staying focused, and highlighting key information is also important.
- Involving subscribers is another aspect that is important. Posing questions, asking them to leave comments, and replying to those comments creates interaction.
- Program or show notes need developing, and they are essential in providing both a summary for the episode along with links to further resources for those interested.
- Evaluation should be done with comprehensive rubrics. Take into account all sides of development: planning, production, and publishing.

In a world where content is increasingly required for just-in-time learning, and knowledge essentially needed only on demand, podcasting and screencasting find themselves extremely conducive for learning. They also offer innovative and creative ways of providing education to students with episode use and production allowing for the development of a broad range of essential life-skills as well as the practice of key second-language skills. This is particularly poignant for the TESOL context as a means of meeting the immediate needs of students, by providing targeted instruction, and would come to enhance the learning experience of all involved.

5. Lesson Plan Guides, and Example Implementation

5. Lesson Plan Guides, and Example Implementation

Provided here are lesson plan guides as well as examples for implementing digital storytelling, Prezi, podcasts and screencasts in the educational context. The guides are meant to assist in the understanding of how to develop a detailed lesson plan, and to help describe what each component and stage of a lesson may cover. The example implementations are intended to provide a use-case scenario detailing the techniques required to apply the use of digital storytelling, Prezi, podcasts and screencasts in real-world settings.

The content covered here includes:

General
- Lesson plan general guide

Digital storytelling
- Lesson plan guide for digital storytelling
- Example implementation: Digital storytelling with fifth-graders in Korea

Prezi
- Lesson plan guide for Prezi in-class creation and development
- Example implementation: Prezi presentation

Podcasting and screencasting
- Lesson plan guide for podcasting
- Example implementation: Podcasting
- Lesson plan guide for screencasting
- Example implementation: Screencasting

Lesson Plan General Guide	
Teaching Context	
Level of Proficiency and Maturity	Student language level (e.g. beginner, intermediate, advanced). Student age range (e.g. young learners, adults).
Lesson Length	Time allotted for the class (e.g. 35-45 minutes).
Lesson Topic	Major theme or focus of the lesson (e.g. numbers and time).
Objectives	Lesson aim (e.g. to teach students how to tell the time and date accurately).
Outcomes	Learning outcomes (e.g. students will be able to read analog and digital timepieces).
Relevant Prior Learning	Anything that students need to know before starting work on this lesson's content (e.g. students need to have completed Chapter Two of the book, and have previously met language associated with appointments, calendars, and timekeeping).

Teacher Preparation	
Hardware	Types of computer or peripherals required (e.g. USB sticks, MP3 players).
Software	Name of software used (e.g. Photo Story 3, Microsoft Word).
Webpage Links	Hyperlink to web resources (e.g. www.google.com).
Additional Resources	Other necessary materials for the lesson (e.g. handouts, worksheets, textbooks).

Procedure			
Stage and Timing	Objective	Teacher	Students
Review Stage (if required, 5 minutes)	Focus of stage (e.g. encourage the use of previously acquired language).	Indicate what the teacher says and does in each stage of the lesson.	Provide expected examples of student behavior.
Warm-up Stage/Pre-Technology Use (10 minutes)	Focus of stage (e.g. introduce new concepts and language to students in a meaningful manner).	Indicate what the teacher says and does in each stage of the lesson.	Provide expected examples of student behavior.
Main Stage/ Technology-based Activity (20 minutes)	Focus of stage (e.g. allow students to utilize technology to become familiar with and apply the concepts and language content introduced in the lesson).	Indicate what the teacher says and does in each stage of the lesson.	Provide expected examples of student behavior.

Practice Stage (15 minutes)	Focus of stage (e.g. allow learners to utilize the skills and language that they are expected to acquire during the lesson in a practical way).	Indicate what the teacher says and does in each stage of the lesson.	Provide expected examples of student behavior.
Lesson Summation Stage/Post-Technology Activities (10 minutes)	Focus of stage (e.g. instructor reinforces the importance of language concepts and skills acquired, stating how they will be useful in future lessons).	Indicate what the teacher says and does in each stage of the lesson.	Provide expected examples of student behavior.

Further Considerations	
Follow-Up Activities	Prepare material that can be applied in a follow up class. Also, be ready with activities for students who complete their class work earlier than expected.
Contingency Plan(s)	Always prepare an alternate teaching scenario in case of any problems. For example, a sudden power outage, or a timetabling issue could make the assigned room unavailable.
Evaluation	Reflect on what worked well, and what did not, and how you might deliver the lesson differently or improve upon it when running it again.

Lesson Plan Guide for Digital Storytelling	
Teaching Context	
Level of Proficiency and Maturity	Beginner to advanced. Adaptable for use with young learners through to adults.
Lesson Length	Several lessons (over a week to a term). Homework completion components. Time allotted for each class: 50 minutes.
Lesson Topic	Variable, from movie reviews to other forms of presentation.
Objectives	1. Enhance communication skills by asking questions, expressing opinions, developing narratives, and writing for an audience. 2. Strengthen media literacy and digital literacy skills (use software, images, audio, video, and other media elements or components).
Outcomes	1. Students will create a structured story (beginning, middle, end). 2. Students employ a range of media to tell their story. 3. Students will show evidence of the ability to express personal opinions.
Relevant Prior Learning	Students will need to be familiar with storytelling components.

Teacher Preparation	
Hardware	Computer or tablet, with internet access and microphone, camera, and scanner (if scanning student work). USB sticks or Google Drive for storage.
Software	Photo Story 3, iMovie, or WeVideo. Microsoft Word or Pages.
Webpage Links	Flickr, Google image search, freemusicarchive.org.
Additional Resources	Storyboarding handout for students to complete offline, and to work on in class.

Procedure – Day 1 of 2			
Stage and Timing	**Objective**	**Teacher**	**Students**
Review Stage (10 minutes)	Remind students of storytelling elements. Ask about stories that they like, start to introduce things that students can talk about in a story (such as their pets).	Teacher directs questions about storytelling (e.g. what students did with their pet on the weekend), prompting responses in a storytelling format.	Students briefly tell about their pet or their weekend in story format, using appropriate sequencers.

Warm-up Stage/Pre-Technology Use (15 minutes)	Introduce the digital storytelling concept.	Play students some appropriate examples from YouTube. Brainstorm story ideas.	Students watch a few examples with a lead to brainstorming ideas.
Main Stage (15 minutes)	Drafting a story can be done on a computer or tablet, or on paper with the handout provided in this book. The focus here is on producing the script for narration.	Assist students on working with the language they need to write their draft, and with the completion of their storyboard.	Students can work together on their story, or they may work individually on their draft to determine the text and sequence.
Lesson Summation Stage/Post-Technology Activities (10 minutes)	Students should be reminded of the lessons goals. The story should have been written by this point, and if not, it can be set for homework completion.	Remind students of what they should have achieved, and ask them to gather music and images for homework.	Students should have completed scripts for narration. Homework will be gathering images and music to match the narration.

Procedure – Day 2 of 2			
Stage and Timing	Objective	Teacher	Students
Review Stage (10 minutes)	Remind students of their homework, and check that it has been completed. Ask students to prepare their materials for digitization.	Teacher directs students to prepare their materials for digitization (this includes images, narrative script/audio, and so on).	Students copy their material from a USB stick, or download it to a computer, tablet or smartphone for sequencing.
Warm-up Stage/Pre-Technology Use (10 minutes)	Materials check, and application preparation.	Ensure student materials match their storyboards, and students are ready to create digital stories using the chosen application.	Students prepare to record their narration and to sequence their story using the appropriate application and content.
Main Stage (20 minutes)	Students use a digital story application to sequence their images, titles, and themes, and then record their narrative script.	Assists students in working on the development of their project, and in the recording of their digital storytelling narrative.	Students successfully sequence their story, and record an appropriate narrative with teacher guidance.

Lesson Summation Stage/Post-Technology Activities (10 minutes)	Students should be able to save their digital storytelling project, and produce a movie file ready for playback. Otherwise, they will need to complete the task for homework.	Ensures students have successfully saved a digital storytelling project file, and are able to produce a movie file for playback by the end of the class period (or are able to do so for homework).	Students complete their digital storytelling project, and produce a movie file that they can share with peers and other stakeholders (such as parents).
Main Stage (20 minutes)	Students use a digital story application to sequence their images, titles, and themes, and then record their narrative script in the target language.	Assists students in working on the development of their digital story project, and in the recording of their narrative.	Students successfully sequence their story, and record an appropriate narrative with teacher guidance.

Lesson Summation Stage/Post-Technology Activities (10 minutes)	Students should be able to save their digital storytelling project, and produce a movie file ready for playback. Otherwise, they will need to complete the task for homework.	Ensures students have successfully saved a digital storytelling project file, and are able to produce a movie file for playback by the end of the class period (or are able to do so for homework).	Students complete their digital storytelling project, and produce a movie file that they can share with peers and other stakeholders (such as parents).

Further Considerations	
Follow-Up Activities	Students can show their movie to peers in the following lesson. This can allow for listening practice, and provide a means to stimulate class cohesion as students gain insight into the language level of their peers as well as their thoughts and interests.
Contingency Plan(s)	The next lesson in the course syllabus should be ready in case there is a problem with using the digital story creation application. Alternatively, some language games can be prepared to fill in the time if technological problems occur. Several activity sheets for review of previous material should be prepared to allow those students who complete their recording to keep busy with language content.
Evaluation	What are the biggest frustrations for implementation? Can these be remedied next time? What are the successes of the lesson? What did students get out of this activity? Can more language practice be provided?

Example Implementation:
Digital Storytelling with Fifth-Graders in Korea

The Teaching and Learning Context

This example centers on an elementary school English club after school activity program, where classes met every Monday to Friday, and every second Saturday, for 40 minutes each time. Teachers were expected to assist students in practicing their language skills, and as there were no exams, they were free to use any resources that they wished. Student language proficiency was ranked as pre-beginner to pre-intermediate according to school conducted level tests. There were twenty students, twelve boys and eight girls, aged 10 to 11, participating in the program. Digital storytelling implementation occurred over six class periods.

Teaching Material

The teaching material can be broken down into three: the software, the hardware, and the book providing learning content.

The software

Microsoft Photo Story (Version 3) was selected and used because

it is free of charge,

it uses a simple wizard to create stories, and

it is very user-friendly (especially for young children).

The hardware

Digitizing tools, such as a scanner and microphone, needed to be readily available so that students could record their narrations, and scan their activity sheets.

Learning content

The sing-along book *Brown Bear, Brown Bear, What do you See?* By Martin & Cale was chosen for pedagogical value, authenticity, and resource availability (such as downloadable coloring activity worksheets). Its rhythmic patterns are helpful and engaging for children on the verge of reading, and it provides just the kind of content that fifth graders can easily manipulate and transfer to a digital storytelling context.

Procedure

Digital storytelling was introduced and implemented with students over a one-week period involving six classes that were held Monday to Saturday and running for 40 minutes each time, thereby providing a total of 240 minutes (four hours) of instruction.

Lesson one – Introducing linguistic content

Overview: Using the Brown Bear text, students were able to become familiar with animal and color vocabulary.

Process: The first class lesson introduced the students to the storybook *Brown Bear, Brown Bear, What Do You See?* and familiarized the class with the linguistic content of the text. This involved introducing students to vocabulary associated with animals and colors. After this, the sing-along storybook was held up for students to see while the instructor read the text, reiterating the animal and color vocabulary in the L1 (first language) where necessary. Follow-up activities involved having students read aloud from a copy of the book, with assistance from the teacher, before progressing to the stage where they were able to read the book aloud on their own.

Lesson two – Introducing a digital version of the text

Overview: Introducing a digital version of the text, as sung by the author of the book and found on YouTube, served to provide review for students.

Process: The second lesson involved presenting a version of the original text as a digital story. This digital story was created by the teacher using a mixture of real animal pictures as well as scanned pictures from the downloadable content available for the book, and this was matched to the text as sung by the author. This step digitizes the initial aspects of the preceding lesson, and provides a 'technology warm-up' activity for students. Students were expected to watch the digital story, and listen to the song. The teacher then reintroduced the animal and color vocabulary, and the digital story was played until all students were able to sing along with the original author of the book as the story progressed.

Lesson three – Solidifying target language vocabulary

Overview: Downloadable coloring activity sheets were provided to students, which also offered color and animal vocabulary practice with cloze exercises.

Process: The third lesson aimed to assist the students in solidifying their knowledge of animal and color vocabulary in English through the use of follow-up coloring activity sheets that were printed from the book website, and were used in the digital story presented in the preceding lesson. As students colored and labeled the black and white pictures of animals from the book, the teacher monitored spelling and vocabulary use, and asked several questions of individuals that involved recall checks (such as "What color is the bear?"), and comprehension checks (such as "What animal is that?"). Students were also encouraged with further vocabulary after prompting with questions (such as "What sound does the animal make?"), and to encourage students in producing English as they worked, the song was played and sung throughout the lesson. It was expected that students would, with teacher assistance, complete the printed activity sheets to a certain standard by the end of the class period, as this material needed to be scanned for use in the following class session.

Lesson four – Whole-class digital storytelling development

Overview: Original content from the sing-along book was used as a retelling task, and as an example of what students would need to create for themselves. The final product was then uploaded to the class website.

Process: The fourth lesson involved the actual introduction and student development of a digital story based on the original sing-along book. For this step, students were able to select and order the scanned activity sheets that they had colored and labeled in the previous lesson so that they matched the order of the song as sung by the book's author. This retelling task was a whole group activity that was completed as students sang the song from memory, prompted as necessary by the teacher. After the correct picture order was achieved, images were imported into the Photo Story 3 program and timed to display with the appropriate song lyrics. The teacher explained the digital storytelling development procedure in a step-by-step fashion, before uploading the story to the class website and informing the students that they would be using the program to create their own story in the following lesson. After uploading the produced digital story to the class website, students reviewed the video and sang along with it.

Lesson five – Practice and reinforcement

Overview: Practice and reinforcement came in the form of students producing a sequenced whole-class digital story that used their own drawings of animals which were labeled and colored accordingly. The final product was also uploaded to the class website before being watched by the class as a whole.

Process: The fifth lesson involved students working on construction of original content for a whole-class produced digital story. They had to draw a picture of an animal different to the animals introduced by the book, label the animal and color it appropriately. They also had to introduce their next classmate's picture in a decided sequence. The instructor monitored this work, assisting as required, and helped each student scan their completed activity sheet. As their activity sheets were scanned, the students read and recorded the text of their labeled image for use as part of the audio portion for the digital story narrative. After all images were scanned and sequenced, and the narrative for each animal recorded, children worked with the practitioner in using Photo Story 3 to solidify their digital storytelling creation knowledge for the next class period. This newly created original digital story was then uploaded to the class website, and watched by the class while reviewing new vocabulary.

Lesson six – Follow-up and individual digital story creation

Overview: Students were expected to create individual digital stories entirely by themselves. At the end of the lesson, each digital story was uploaded to the class website to share with parents and peers before being watched together as a class.

Process: In the final lesson, as a follow-up step, students were expected to develop a complete digital story entirely by themselves. This involved drawing, coloring, and labeling several activity sheets to form a scanned sequence, recording matching audio narration, and using Photo Story 3 to produce content in a movie-file format that could be then published on the class website. Throughout this process, the teacher supported the students as they worked, providing technical and linguistic assistance and encouragement as required. At the end of the lesson, each of these digital stories was uploaded to the class website to share with parents and peers before being watched together as a class.

Lesson Plan Guide for Prezi In-Class Creation and Development	
Teaching Context	
Level of Proficiency and Maturity	Beginner to advanced. Adaptable for use with young learners through to adults.
Lesson Length	Several lessons (over a week to a term). Homework completion components. Time allotted for each class: 50 minutes.
Lesson Topic	Variable, from portfolio compilation to single topic presentation.
Objectives	1. Enhance communication skills by expressing opinions on a topic, developing presentation skills, and writing for an audience. 2. Strengthen media literacy and digital literacy skills (use software, images, audio, video, and other media elements or components).
Outcomes	1. Students will create a multimedia-based presentation. 2. Students will employ a range of media resources during their presentation. 3. Students will show evidence of the ability to express personal opinions on a topic.
Relevant Prior Learning	Students will need to be familiar with mind mapping.

Teacher Preparation	
Hardware	Computer or tablet, with internet access and microphone, camera, and scanner (if scanning resources). USB sticks or Google Drive for storage of resources if needed.
Software	Microsoft Word (if mind mapping and note-taking). Prezi.
Webpage Links	Prezi, Flickr, Google image search, freemusicarchive.org.
Additional Resources	Prezi Presentation Preparation handout for students to complete offline, and to work on in class.

Procedure – Day 1 of 2			
Stage and Timing	Objective	Teacher	Students
Review Stage (10 minutes)	Remind students of the elements that make a good presentation. Reintroduce the concept of mind mapping and note-taking for developing a presentation topic.	Teacher elicits information from students by asking questions (e.g. what makes a good presentation? How do you make a mind map?) responses are written on board.	Students should be able to provide several examples of how to give a presentation, and describe the process of how to create a mind map.
Warm-up Stage/Pre-Technology Use (15 minutes)	Introduce the Prezi presentation paradigm.	Show at least one example Prezi as a best practice model.	Students are introduced to a few sample Prezis.

Main Stage (15 minutes)	Develop an initial Prezi with students using the Prezi practice exercise and tutorial handout.	Work through the handout with students, helping them to develop their first Prezi. Introduce new vocabulary as required.	Students work with the teacher, and together, develop an initial Prezi.
Lesson Summation Stage/Post-Technology Activities (10 minutes)	Students should be reminded of the lesson goals, and can be invited to select and show important components of a Prezi, and illustrate the view path.	Remind students of what they should have achieved, help them identify key elements of a Prezi, and ask them to gather resources and a topic idea to create a Prezi of their own for homework.	Students should have a good understanding of the workings of a Prezi, and be able to use the Prezi presentation preparation handout to help them develop an initial outline for a Prezi topic.

Procedure – Day 2 of 2			
Stage and Timing	Objective	Teacher	Students
Review Stage (10 minutes)	Remind students of their homework, and check that it has been adequately completed.	Teacher ensures that an outline of a Prezi presentation has been developed with an associated view path, and that it can be presented in the chosen time frame.	Students have prepared an initial outline and rudimentary view path for their presentation using the homework handout.
Warm-up Stage/Pre-Technology Use (10 minutes)	Elements of presenting and associated vocabulary need to be introduced to students.	The teacher ensures that students understand how to give a presentation, and are aware of the importance of aspects such as body language and voice projection.	Students come to understand that they are the focal point of the presentation, and that the Prezi provides multimedia-based support for their presentation.
Main Stage (20 minutes)	Students use the Prezi presentation preparation handout to finalize their presentation topic.	The teacher assists students in the development of student Prezis, as well as in the writing of any accompanying presentation material.	Students successfully sequence their view path, place their resources, and create matching notes.

Lesson Summation Stage/Post-Technology Activities (10 minutes)	Students should have completed their Prezi development, and be able to export or share it. Otherwise, they will need to complete this task for homework.	Ensures that students have successfully saved or exported a complete Prezi (or are able to do so for homework).	Students complete their Prezi, and produce associated notes to speak along with the presentation. The Prezi should also be exported or saved to share with peers and other stakeholders (e.g. parents).

Further Considerations	
Follow-Up Activities	Students present their Prezi to peers in a following lesson. To do this, students implement the methods that they have been taught to rely on when giving a presentation (for example, using body language and voice projection), and be provided with an appropriate rubric if the Prezi presentation is to be assessed. Audience members should be prepared to ask one question of the presenter.
Contingency Plan(s)	The handout used in the lesson summation post-technology activity can be extended, and used to fill a full class hour. However, if this is not used at this time, then the next lesson in the course syllabus should be ready in case there is a problem with using the Prezi website or other technology. Alternatively, some language games can be prepared to fill in the time if technological problems occur.
Evaluation	What are the biggest frustrations for implementation? Can these be remedied next time? What are the successes of the lesson? What did students get out of this activity? Can more language practice be provided?

Example Implementation:
Prezi Presentation

The Teaching and Learning Context

Prezi can be applied by any teacher who requires their students to develop a multimedia-based presentation. It could be associated with language point reviews with younger learners (for example, presenting idioms and their meanings), the results of collaborative projects with older learners (for example, presenting a demonstration or tutorial), or even job roles when used with adult students (for example, presenting the work-related life of a bank teller). As such, the method of implementation would be well suited for any school, subject, or grade-level. Suitability for use with second-language learners is dependent only upon the teacher's ability to adapt the material to the teaching and learning context, which means that you should ensure that the topic is relevant to both the students' needs and interests.

Teaching Material

The teaching material required can be broken down under three headings: the software, the hardware, and a variety of media resources that students have chosen to use throughout their presentation as learning content.

The software

The Prezi presentation software will be required. It is browser-based, and will need to be used while connected to the internet. Its application for a range of devices can also be downloaded to view and to show a Prezi as required.

The hardware

The minimum hardware required is a device that can access the internet using a web browser, but a built-in microphone may be necessary if students want to record themselves. You will also need a scanner if students wish to scan in samples of their own work, or other offline material, for digitalization.

Learning content

Learning content will stem from students developing a Prezi presentation that comes to revolve around the incorporation of various multimedia elements. These elements could possibly consist of a variety of media, from videos and photographs taken on smartphones to hand-drawn images, and from student-recorded voice through to copyright-free music. The content can already be in a digital format, or it might need to be digitalized.

Procedure

A Prezi presentation can be given and graded, much like any other, such as one that uses Microsoft PowerPoint or Apple Keynote. However, providing a Prezi presentation outline that students can use to help build their own Prezi presentation is perhaps one of the best ways to incorporate the use of the Prezi presentation paradigm in your classes. Why? Because you will be able to provide a tutorial in the use of the software while simultaneously introducing students to the steps that they will need to conduct to complete the presentation task satisfactorily. It will also provide second-language learners with additional language practice as you model the expected task outcomes for them. The topic or content behind the presentation may also see students being able to establish a more personal connection with you, especially if the topic is one that involves their interests such as hobbies and family.

Step one – Identify

Identify the type of assignment or work that you will have your students turn into a presentation. Also, identify if the topic is best suited for in-class work or homework, and for students to work on individually, in pairs, or as a group. Further, depending on the teaching context and the age of students, it might be advisable to have each student initially present solo or on a topic that they are familiar with (for example, themselves, a place, or a favorite thing), then later work collaboratively on a presentation surrounding an unfamiliar topic that would require research (for example, explaining vocabulary or idioms, providing a tutorial, or giving a demonstration).

Step two – Familiarize

Provide examples, and ensure that students are familiar with how to design a Prezi, and how to use the software to create a multimedia-based presentation. To this end, develop a Prezi of your own following a similar topic that you will want students to provide a presentation on. Then, work with students to explain how to use the software while building a template or outline that students can then later use as a model to follow when beginning work on their own presentations or when working with peers.

Step three – Develop

Ensure that each student has access to the completed outline that was built as part of the Prezi tutorial. This is worthwhile as it ensures that all students have the same template to work from, and provides a framework to begin to integrate content in order to build a final presentation for delivery. It will also be less time-consuming for students to develop a presentation from an outline, so focus can be placed more on actual language use as well as the development of multimedia-based items for inclusion in the project. It also provides students with a precise format to follow (so it is teacher-guided), and with motivation to include or develop the appropriate content (so it is student-centered).

Step four – Present

The Prezi presentation paradigm allows for both on and offline presentation as well as submission as homework or for delivery as an in-class presentation. Each of these presentation options will depend on the specific teaching and learning context as well as the topic, but if delivered as an in-class presentation, then it will help build learner confidence as students start to use the language that they have learned in front of others while sharing their own ideas and thoughts (be they professional or personal ones). This in turn can also make the language learning process more personal and more interesting.

Step five – Grade and give feedback

Providing appropriate and timely feedback is also important. You should be prepared to use an evaluation rubric, such as one that can be found in this book, and to give feedback not only on the presentation itself but also on the students' English language abilities (pronunciation, grammar, vocabulary), body language (gestures, stance), and voice projection. Also consider whether this feedback should be given publicly or privately.

Step six – Distribute

If desired, the Prezi can be shared on social media, or embedded within a class blog post or a page on a learning management system (LMS) such as Moodle. Each presentation would then be available for all students to review as required, and for other stakeholders (such as parents and administration) to view at leisure.

Lesson Plan Guide for Podcasting	
Teaching Context	
Level of Proficiency and Maturity	Beginner to advanced. Adaptable for use with young learners through to adults.
Lesson Length	Suitable for several lessons over a week. Homework completion components. Time allotted for each class: 50 minutes.
Lesson Topic	Variable, anything suited to a commercial radio broadcast would work well, particularly talkback interviews.
Objectives	1. Enhance communication skills through collaborative learning, asking questions, expressing opinions, and developing scripts. 2. Strengthen multiple literacies (computer literacy, digital literacy, and English literacy).
Outcomes	1. Students identify significant questions on a topic, and use these in interview format. 2. Transfer current knowledge into learning, using and understanding technological systems.
Relevant Prior Learning	None required. Screencasting or digital storytelling familiarity helpful.

Teacher Preparation	
Hardware	Computer or tablet with audio recording capability (e.g. built-in or external microphone). USB sticks or Google Drive for storage.
Software	Podcasting software (e.g. Audacity)
Webpage Links	Podgallery
Additional Resources	Handouts*: • Podcast summary and review • Podcast design plan • Podcasting production plan • Podcast show notes

*Available under 'Photocopiable material'.

Procedure – Day 1 of 3			
Stage and Timing	**Objective**	**Teacher**	**Students**
Introductory Stage (5 minutes)	Determine student familiarity with podcasts, and find out what students like to listen to on the radio.	Determine student familiarity with podcasts by introducing radio shows, and downloadable and streaming programs (e.g. from Podgallery, or other sources).	Express opinions about the radio shows that they like to listen to, download or stream.
Warm-up Stage/Pre-Technology Use (5 minutes)	Brainstorm good topics for podcasts, and provide links to examples of suitable podcasts.	Help students think of topics that they can later use to make their own podcasts, and provide links to suitable examples.	Students start to think about topics that are suitable for podcasts, and they are introduced to some that they can listen to later.

Main Stage (20 minutes)	Play an interview type podcast to students, suitable to their language level.	Play a short podcast to students, at a maximum of three times, and have them complete the 'Podcast Summary and Review' handout*.	Students will listen to the podcast, and complete the associated handout.
Lesson Summation Stage/Post-Technology Activities (10 minutes)	Go through the worksheet answers with students, and remind them of podcasts that are suitable for language learning.	Go over the worksheet with students, and check answers. Finish the lesson by providing several podcast links.	Students are provide their answers from the worksheet, and are provided with podcast links that they can use to improve their English.

*Available under 'Photocopiable material'.

Procedure – Day 2 of 3			
Stage and Timing	**Objective**	**Teacher**	**Students**
Review Stage (5 minutes)	Remind students of podcasts, types of podcasts, and the structure of a podcast.	Introduce the structure of podcasts by talking through the handouts*: 'podcast design plan' and 'podcast production plan'.	Students become familiar with the structure and planning process behind the production of a podcast.
Warm-up Stage/Pre-Technology Use (5 minutes)	Help students choose a podcast topic that would suit an interview format.	Brainstorm several topics for a podcast based on unit topics (e.g. a movie unit, an interview with a celebrity).	Students brainstorm several ideas for a podcast that they will design and produce, either in pairs or in small groups.

*Available under 'Photocopiable material'.

Main Stage (35 minutes)	Students begin to develop notes for their script.	Help students to work through the handouts to develop their podcast content. Assign a maximum time for the podcast (e.g. 5 or 10 minutes).	Students work through the handouts to develop their podcast design plan, interview questions, and the roles of each student if the task is group work.
Lesson Summation Stage/Post-Technology Activities (5 minutes)	Inform students that they will record their podcast in the next class session.	Tell students that they will record their podcast in the next class session. So, their handouts must be complete and scripts and interview questions ready.	Students will complete the handouts and develop show notes for homework if these have not been completed during class time.

Procedure – Day 3 of 3			
Stage and Timing	**Objective**	**Teacher**	**Students**
Review Stage (5 minutes)	Go over the previous class content (handouts).	Confirm that students have completed their handouts, and are ready to record their podcast with a completed script.	Scripts and show notes should be fully developed, and the podcast production checklist complete.
Warm-up Stage/Pre-Technology Use (10 minutes)	Provide time for students to practice reading their podcasts together.	Check student scripts, show notes, and interview questions. Also check that these will meet the previously assigned time limit for the podcast.	Students practice reading their podcasts aloud together.

Main Stage (20 minutes)	Record the podcast.	Assist students in recording the podcast using the appropriate hardware.	Students record their podcast as an MP3, and convert show notes to a PDF.
Lesson Summation Stage/Post-Technology Activities (10 minutes)	Upload podcasts, and show notes to a selected site.	Help students to finalize their content, and upload it to a selected site (such as a class blog).	Students finalize their podcast, and show notes, and upload these to the internet.

Further Considerations	
Follow-Up Activities	Students working in groups can produce several podcasts that can be played back to the class as a 'presentation', with the summary and review worksheets used to keep students focused on listening. These can then be evaluated using rubrics like those given throughout this book.
Contingency Plan(s)	The next lesson in the course syllabus should be ready in case there is a problem at any stage of podcast development. Alternatively, some language games can be prepared to fill in the time if technological problems occur. Several activity sheets for review of previous material should be prepared to allow those students who complete their scripts or recording to keep busy with language content.
Evaluation	What are the biggest frustrations for implementation? Can these be remedied next time? What are the successes of the lesson? What did students get out of this activity? Can more language practice be provided?

Example Implementation: Podcasting

The Teaching and Learning Context

The example podcast presented here could be used either as a homework task, or used in-class as a short introduction or as a review for listening. Podcasts like this one are designed to be short listening exercises that a teacher may wish to include routinely with a number of episodes created over a school term or year, and specifically to engage students in review. It is suitable for middle school students through to adults who are studying general English, and it illustrates the steps required to design and deliver a podcast that could be used with all levels of learners. The associated worksheets, and any related articles or links provided in the show notes can be adapted as needed.

Teaching Material

The teaching material can be broken down into three: the software, the hardware, and the worksheets required to develop and deliver the learning content.

The software

To engage in the production of a podcast, a reliable means of editing, producing, and saving the recordings locally, finding a place to host the recordings, transcripts, and show notes on the internet, and determining a means for distributing the recordings via RSS is essential. A recommendation for teachers who are just starting out with podcasting is to use: Audacity (for editing and recording), Dragon Naturally Speaking (for any necessary transcription), Weebly or WordPress (for hosting show notes, and the podcast files themselves), and FETCHRSS: RSS Generator (to create an RSS feed for the webpage where your files are located). Ultimately, the choice of editing tool, hosting service, and feed creator is yours, and from the many available, you will need to become familiar with the nuances of those that you select.

The hardware

Several hardware items are required to physically record a podcast before it can be edited, distributed, and turned into effective learning content. At minimum, this would include a device capable of recording audio, and then being able to upload this to a hosting service and create an RSS feed. It is strongly recommended that an external microphone with a pop filter and a quit location be used to perform the recording.

Learning content

A number of worksheets are required in order to smoothly create a podcast for educational purposes. These include one to establish a design plan for the podcast that you intend to produce, which would then allow you to work out the production steps and a potential script that can then be turned into a transcript for inclusion with the show notes. Once the podcast has been recorded, the show notes then need to be developed, along with a complete transcript of the recording. At this stage a worksheet or two can be developed for student use, either in association with listening to the podcast at home for homework or in-class as an introductory or a review exercise undertaken with teacher guidance. The audio file, the transcript, and show notes can then be hosted on the internet, and distributed through RSS.

The worksheets mentioned here have been completed with a sample podcast for use with students, and they include:
- the podcasting design plan
- the podcast production steps
- the podcast transcript

- the podcast show notes
- the podcast student worksheet (one and two)

Procedure

The worksheets provided here are presented as example implementation methods, and are meant to illustrate how a podcast can be planned, produced, transcribed, and then turned into learning content. You can modify this classroom content for use with your students. The worksheets are intended to be used in stages, as outlined on the following pages:

Stage one – Development

In the podcast development stage, you will need to focus on the unit and lesson that the podcast may be used for, and on the topic and language points that might be imparted through it. Keeping these aspects in mind, the design plan and the production step worksheets can then be completed. The worksheets that are provided as examples look at accompanying a unit on *'comparing and contrasting'*, and seek to provide familiarity with the expression *'on the other hand ...'*, while using a topic familiar to most students the home.

Stage two – Content creation

After the production and planning stage comes the need to meet with a guest – that is, if the interview mode has been chosen as the most appropriate for the podcast. The show can then be recorded using the questions developed in the scripting section of the production plan, and edited, with music and transitions placed appropriately. A transcript can then be created using voice recognition software, along with show notes. The files can then be hosted, and a distribution feed created. At this point, the language learning content can then be developed, based on the final product, with student worksheets can be created.

Stage three – Student use

The podcast provided could be set for in-class listening at either the beginning or the end of a unit, as it is intended to serve as an introductory or a review piece. Alternatively, it may also be used as a time-filler or be set for homework. The listening portion of the podcast should play for around 5 to 7 minutes when fully produced with music and audio transitions. The associated student worksheets include listening and post-listening tasks, and would take around 30 minutes or so to go over and complete if the podcast is played three times.

Podcast Design Plan	
Podcast Title	**Group Members**
A new place.	Teacher.
Guest(s) Murray Cod, a student from our school.	
Topic	**Unit/Lesson** Comparing and contrasting
Objectives	1. Identify, become familiar with, and be able to use the expression '*on the other hand*'. 2. Identify and define any unfamiliar expressions or vocabulary (for example, '*got you*', '*character*', and '*digs*').
Planning	**Intent of broadcast** Language practice **Length of broadcast** 5-7 minutes **Number of episodes** 1 **Style of recording** Interview **Recording location** On campus
Producing	**Hardware required** iPad. ☑Hardware is operational ☑ Hardware is usable ☑ Production plan developed*
Publishing	☑ Files hosted ☑ RSS Feed created **Show notes link** www.mycasts.net/snotes001 **Transcript link** www.mycasts.net/transcript001
Promoting	**Listener involvement** Ask listener's to leave comments/questions; provide links to articles (how to hose a housewarming, how to decorate a new place) and any mentioned while recording. **Links spread to** Facebook and school website.

Podcast Production Plan	
Introductory Music (30-60 seconds)	"Another word on the board" by The Chalk Dusters
Introductory Monologue (30-60 seconds)	Welcome back to another episode of the Teaching with Technology podcast: the place to go for all your language learning needs. I'm your host Noah Tall. Today we will be talking with Murray Cod, a student at our school, and finding out a little about his move into new accommodation.
Topics (3-5 minutes each)	1. A new place, with guest, Murray Cod.
Closing Remarks (2 minutes)	Cheers, Murray. Now, don't forget to check out our show notes, and leave a question or comment to tell us what you think about the show. Catch us next week when one of the school's faculty members is going to drop by and provide some study tips that might help you to ace that next exam. I'm Dr. Noah Tall, and this has been another Teaching with Technology podcast.
Closing Music (2 minutes)	"Another word on the board" by The Chalk Dusters

Podcast Transcript

Host: Welcome back to another episode of the Teaching with Technology podcast: the place to go for all your language learning needs. I'm your host Noah Tall. Today we will be talking with Murray Cod, a student at our school, and finding out a little about his move into new accommodation. So, welcome to the show Murray. You're a student here at our school, and it's good to talk with you today. Please introduce yourself to our listeners.

Guest: Thank you, sir. Yes, I've been attending this school for over six months now, but I used to find it a little difficult to get to classes on time because I lived so far away.

Host: Yes, I'm sure many of our students might find that familiar. I'm guessing that a lot of our students take public transport too. Was it always running late? Is that what made you late to class?

Guest: Sometimes, but I would usually check the 'Klickety-Klack' transport app to find out if the buses were on time or not. So that wasn't really the problem.

Host: I see. We'll put a link to that app in the show notes in case some students here are not familiar with it. So, if the transport isn't so much the problem, then it sounds like maybe a few late nights then?

Guest: Er, maybe. (*Laughs*)

Host: Well, you were up studying of course. No, I got you. Hey, you know this all really leads us into our topic for today. We are going to be talking about your new accommodation. So, it sounds like you have just moved into a new place?

Guest: Indeed, I have. About two weeks ago? Yeah, two weeks ago. I've been living in my new place now for two weeks.

Host: Great. So tell me, what are the main differences between your old place and the new one?

Guest: Probably the biggest difference is that the old place is a lot more modern than the new place.

Host: Okay, so the old place is more modern. On the other hand, the new place has a lot more character, right?

Guest: Well, yes, you could say that. The old place is also lot further away, and it just took way too long to get to school. I didn't like that at all.

Host: That's great to hear. How about the size of the old and new places? Is the new place much bigger?

Guest: Yes, a little bigger, and there are more rooms. I now have a room that I can use just for study.

Host: And the rent?

Guest: Oh, yeah. The rent is a lot cheaper near the school. I will say though, the old place, although more expensive, is more conveniently located to shops. On the other hand, I can now walk to school from the new place so that can save on daily public transport costs.

Host: So, where did you hear about this new place?

Guest: Well, I just spotted a realtor near the west gate bus stop. 'Around Town' Realty is their name, and they had a lot of pretty nice and reasonably priced apartments available near school. It was pretty easy actually.

Host: Yeah, it sounds like it. I'm glad that you're liking your new digs, and we will put a link to that realtor's home page in our show notes – in case anyone else out there is thinking about making a move to a place that's a little closer to school. Also, it seems to be about time to close our episode for today, and say goodbye to listeners for another week. Thank you for dropping by to talk with us, Murray.

Guest: Thank you, and goodbye listeners.

Host: Cheers, Murray! Now, don't forget to check out our show notes, and leave a question or comment to tell us what you think about the show. Catch us next week when one of the school's faculty members is going to drop by and provide some study tips that might help you to ace that next exam. I'm Dr. Noah Tall, and this has been another Teaching with Technology podcast.

Teaching with Technology Podcast **Show Notes**
Podcast title A new place. **Air date** 03/03/17. **Guest(s)** Murray Cod, a student at our school.
Podcast/Screencast overview We find out about an app that may get you to school on time, meet a new student from our school who talks with us a little about his new place, and find out where to go to rent an apartment near campus.
Episode highlights *We meet Murray Cod, a student at our school.* [00:40] *Murray talks about using the 'Klickety-Klack' app.* [01:33] *Murray starts to compare his old place to his new place.* [02:30] *Murray tells us how he found his new place.* [04:30]

Resources from this episode
   1.   The 'Klickety-Klack' app for Android.
   2.   The 'Klickety-Klack' app for iOS.
   3.   The 'Around Town Realty' home page.

Related articles
   1.   How to host a housewarming.
   2.   How to decorate a new place.

Teaching with Technology Podcast
Student Worksheet 1

Instructions

Listen to the latest episode of the teaching with technology podcast.

1. First listening – Listening for the topic

As you listen, try to understand as much as you can and identify the topic.

Q. Which sentence below matches best with the topic of the podcast:

☐ The podcast is about public transport.

☐ The podcast is about comparing a new place to an old one.

☐ The podcast is about study tips to help you ace an exam.

2. Second listening – Listening for detail

As you listen, try to catch as many details as you can and place a tick (✓) in the correct column.

Which place ...	New Place	Old Place
... is more modern?		
... is bigger?		
... has higher rent?		
... has more rooms?		
... is closer to school?		

(Use with Worksheet Two)

Teaching with Technology Podcast
Student Worksheet 2

3. Third listening – Listening for expressions and vocabulary

As you listen, pay close attention to any words or phrases that may be new to you. Try to write down as many as you can, and then try to decide what they might mean.

New word/expression	Possible meaning
1. _____	_____
2. _____	_____
3. _____	_____
4. _____	_____
5. _____	_____
6. _____	_____

4. After listening – What about you?

Now think about where you live. What things are important or not important to you? Tick (✓) the appropriate column.

My place ...	Important	Not Important
is modern		
is big		
has low rent		
has many rooms		
is close to school/work		
is near to shops		
is near public transport		

(Use with Worksheet One)

Lesson Plan Guide for Screencasting	
Teaching Context	
Level of Proficiency and Maturity	Beginner to advanced. Adaptable for use with young learners through to adults.
Lesson Length	Suitable for several lessons over a week. Homework completion components. Time allotted for each class: 50 minutes.
Lesson Topic	Variable. Anything suited to a demonstration, procedure, or tutorial would work well (e.g. how to create a glog using Glogster).
Objectives	1. Enhance communication skills through collaborative learning, demonstrations, and script development. 2. Strengthen multiple literacies (computer literacy, digital literacy, and English literacy).
Outcomes	1. Students identify significant points on a topic, and use these in a tutorial. 2. Transfer current knowledge into learning and the use and understanding of technological systems.
Relevant Prior Learning	None required. Podcasting or digital storytelling experience helpful.

Teacher Preparation	
Hardware	Computer or tablet with audio recording capability (e.g. built-in or external microphone). USB sticks or Google Drive for storage.
Software	Screencasting software (e.g. Screencast-O-Matic)
Webpage Links	Screencast-O-Matic screencast.com
Additional Resources	Handouts*: • Screencast summary and review • Screencast design plan • Screencasting production plan • Screencast show notes

*Available under 'Photocopiable material'.

Procedure – Day 1 of 3			
Stage and Timing	**Objective**	**Teacher**	**Students**
Introductory Stage **(5 minutes)**	Determine student familiarity with screencasts, and find out what tutorial type videos students have watched.	Determine student familiarity with screencasts by introducing examples (e.g. from Screencast.com or YouTube).	Express opinions about the video tutorials they have used in the past.
Warm-up Stage/Pre-Technology Use **(5 minutes)**	Brainstorm good topics for screencasts, provide links to examples of suitable tutorial type screencasts.	Help students to think of topics that they can later use to make their own screencasts, and provide links to suitable examples.	Students start to think about the topics suitable for screencasts, and are introduced to some screencasts that they can watch later.

Main Stage (20 minutes)	Play a tutorial type podcast to students, that is suitable to their language level.	Play a short screencast to students, at a maximum of three times, and have them complete the 'Screencast Summary and Review' handout*.	Students will watch the screencast, and complete the associated handout.
Lesson Summation Stage/Post-Technology Activities (10 minutes)	Go through the worksheet answers with students, and remind them of screencasts that are suitable for language learning.	Go over the worksheet with students, and check their answers. Finish the lesson by providing several links for students to watch in their own time.	Students are called on to provide their answers from the worksheet, and are provided with suitable screencast links that they can use to improve their English.

*Available under 'Photocopiable material'.

Procedure – Day 2 of 3			
Stage and Timing	Objective	Teacher	Students
Review Stage (5 minutes)	Remind students of screencasts, the types of screencast, and the structure of a screencast.	Introduce the structure of screencasts by talking through the handouts*: 'screencast design plan' and 'screencast production plan'.	Students become familiar with the structure and planning process behind the production of a screencast.
Warm-up Stage/Pre-Technology Use (5 minutes)	Help students choose a screencast topic that would suit a tutorial format.	Brainstorm several topics for a screencast that is based on unit topics (e.g. demonstration speech unit, how to make a glog on Glogster).	Students brainstorm several ideas for a screencast that they will design and produce in pairs or in small groups.

*Available under 'Photocopiable material'.

Main Stage (35 minutes)	Students begin to develop notes for their script.	Help students to work through the handouts to develop their screencast content. Assign a maximum time for the screencast (e.g. 5 or 10 minutes).	Students work through the handouts to develop their screencast design plan, script, and the roles of each student if the task is group work.
Lesson Summation Stage/Post-Technology Activities (5 minutes)	Inform students that they will record their screencast in the next class session. This will require all students have access to a computer or a device to allow for this to occur.	Tell students that they will record their screencast in the next class session. This means that their handouts must be complete and their scripts are ready.	Students will complete the handouts and develop program notes for homework if these have not been completed during class time.

Procedure – Day 3 of 3			
Stage and Timing	**Objective**	**Teacher**	**Students**
Review Stage (5 minutes)	Go over the previous class content (handouts).	Confirm that students have completed their handouts, and are ready to record their screencast with a completed script.	Scripts and program notes should be fully developed, and the screencast production checklist complete.
Warm-up Stage/Pre-Technology Use (10 minutes)	Provide time for students to practice reading their screencasts together.	Check student scripts, show notes, and interview questions. Also check that these will meet the previously assigned time limit for the screencast.	Students practice reading their screencasts aloud together.

Main Stage (20 minutes)	Record the screencast.	Assist students in recording the screencast using the appropriate software.	Students record their screencast as an MP4, and convert program notes to a PDF.
Lesson Summation Stage/Post-Technology Activities (10 minutes)	Upload screencasts and program notes to a selected site.	Help students to finalize their content, and upload it to a selected site (such as a class blog, or YouTube).	Students finalize their screencast and program notes, and upload these to the internet.

Further Considerations	
Follow-Up Activities	Students working in groups can produce several screencasts that can be played back to the class as a kind of presentation, with the summary and review worksheets used to keep the other students focused. These can then be evaluated using rubrics like those found throughout this book. Students can be assigned homework, and work as pairs, to make screencast vocabulary flashcards as a way to review important vocabulary.
Contingency Plan(s)	The next lesson in the course syllabus should be ready in case there is a problem at any stage of screencast development. Alternatively, some language games can be prepared to fill in the time if technological problems occur. Several activity sheets for review of previous material should be prepared to allow those students who complete their scripts or recording to keep busy with language content.
Evaluation	What are the biggest frustrations for implementation? Can these be remedied next time? What are the successes of the lesson? What did students get out of this activity? Can more language practice be provided?

Example Implementation:
Screencasting

The Teaching and Learning Context

The example of screencast use here could be applied by any teacher when grading a student's homework. The method of implementation would be well suited for any school, subject, or grade-level of students. Its suitability for use with second-language learners is dependent only on the teacher's ability to adapt the use of their language to suit the level of their learners as they conduct the screencast. If you are using this model with your students to deliver feedback on writing, or adapting it work with other kinds of electronic submissions, then you would need to adapt your language use based on your knowledge of the students.

Descriptive Feedback

Descriptive feedback should be designed to help learners adjust what they are doing so that they can improve (Davies, 2007), and it should therefore help students identify what they are doing well, what areas they might need to cultivate, and what steps they may be able to take to develop themselves. The feedback should be clear, specific, meaningful, and timely.

It is important to consider several factors when conducting descriptive feedback, including the timing of when it is provided, the amount, the way it is provided, and who it is going to be provided to.

Timing

Provide feedback as often as possible: immediately for something that is right or wrong; later if a comprehensive review is needed (but not too long so that it would not make a difference).

Amount

Prioritize the most important points for feedback.

Select points that are reflective of learning goals.

Consider student level when grading.

Mode

Immediate feedback may be best in person, or in passing students on a classroom walk-around.

Interactive feedback, talking directly with one student at a time, may be best for feedback on spoken tasks.

Written feedback may be best on written work.

Demonstrations could be required to ensure students know how to perform a task.

Audience

Individual feedback may see students respond by thinking "the teacher values me".

Group/whole-class feedback may be best when all or most students require the same feedback: good or bad (for example, praise on completing a task effectively, or a language point that all students need consistent correction on).

Descriptive Feedback Model for Screencasting

Providing a screencast while conducting descriptive grading of student submissions is perhaps one of the best ways to incorporate the use of screencasting in your classes. This is because you will be able to perform the integration of technology and screencast use without much additional time allotted to carrying out the task. It will also provide second-language learners with additional language practice, as you model good work for them, as well as allowing them to establish a more personal connection with you as their teacher.

Teaching Material

The teaching material required can be broken down into three: the software, the hardware, and the student work that requires grading.

The software

Any screencasting software can be used for providing feedback on student produced digital content. One option might be Screen-O-Matic as it can be used browser-based or installed locally.

The hardware

The minimum hardware required is a device that can run the software that you have chosen to use for screencasting, and has either a built-in microphone or a means to connect an external microphone (one with a pop filter). You could also need a scanner if seeking to screencast non-digitized content.

Learning content

The learning content in this context is any student-produced content that can be graded. The content can be either already in a digital format, and returned in digital form with feedback, or it can be digitalized.

Procedure

The type of content that is being graded will reflect on how you annotate the material and dictate feedback. For example, if you are using Microsoft Word files, then you will be able to use features such as 'Track changes' along with notes, and explain why these are being changed or added as you screencast. Other options are using a 'Note' program to add sticky notes to content as you grade or keep a rolling list of comments. You may also simply use the mouse as a pointer to highlight areas of focus, and provide spoken feedback regarding any points of note. In any of these cases, all of the steps below are similar, and they are suitable to follow for the screencasting of descriptive feedback of any student-produced content.

Step one – Identify

Identify the type of assignment or work that you will conduct your descriptive feedback on (for example, blog post, digital story, essay, glog poster, or slideshow presentation).

Step two – Select

Select the application to conduct the screencast, and open student work that is ready for grading.

Step three - Grade

Grade your students' work as you normally would, and during the time that is normally allotted for conducting such a task, except dictate feedback as you annotate and highlight the aspects of students' work that needs correcting, praising, or improving. Working with content that has not yet been digitialized may require the scanning of student worksheets into a single PDF, and then developing a screencast that goes through this file while grading, annotating, and dictating. Alternatively, a web camera could be used that captures the hardcopy content physically being graded along with the teacher comments, so that annotations could be made directly onto students' work, and then returned to them.

Step four – Distribute

Save and upload the screencast as a single file for each student, or as a single file containing all of the students' feedback. In either case, it would then be available for each student and stakeholder, as well as a whole-class review when required.

6. Photocopiable Material

6. Photocopiable Material

This section contains photocopiable content, and you are free to make as many copies as you require for teaching purposes and preparing your classes. Any other use or distribution should include a citation to the source of the content. In developing your digital stories, Prezis, podcasts and screencasts, it will prove useful to use the provided resource notes and handouts as a guide.

The lesson plan template can be used for considering how best to integrate the steps for using digital stories, Prezis, podcasts and screencasts with your classes. As such, the template is meant to act as a means to think about how to implement, with your classes, aspects of what has been discovered through this book. The template should be supplemented with any necessary material, along with the staging as well as other aspects of the lesson being adjusted as required.

The following photocopiable material is available:

General
- Lesson plan template

Digital storytelling
- Digital storytelling storyboarding resource notes
- Digital storytelling storyboarding handout

Prezi
- Prezi presentation preparation resource notes
- Prezi presentation preparation handout
- Prezi practice exercise and tutorial
- Prezi presentation tips

Podcasting and screencasting
- Podcast design plan resource notes
- Podcast design plan handout
- Podcast production plan resource notes
- Podcast production plan handout
- Screencast design plan resource notes
- Screencast design plan handout
- Screencast production plan resource notes
- Screencast production plan handout
- Podcast/Screencast summary and review resource notes
- Podcast/Screencast summary and review handout
- Podcast/Screencast show/program notes resource notes
- Podcast/Screencast show/program notes handout

Lesson Plan Template	
Teaching Context	
Level of Proficiency and Maturity	
Lesson Length	
Lesson Topic	
Objectives	
Outcomes	
Relevant Prior Learning	
Teacher Preparation	
Hardware	
Software	
Webpage Links	
Additional Resources	

Procedure			
Stage and Timing	Objective	Teacher	Students
Review Stage (if required)			
Warm-up Stage/Pre-Technology Use			
Main Stage/ Technology-based Activity			
Practice Stage			
Lesson Summation Stage/Post-Technology Activities			

Further Considerations	
Follow-Up Activities	
Contingency Plan(s)	
Evaluation	

Digital Storytelling Storyboarding Resource Notes		
Digital Story Title A title is chosen by students, and written here.		**Group Members** Student names are listed here.
Image Students sketch an example image (or paste one) here that reflects what will appear at this point in their digital story.	**Description** Students will answer one or all of the following questions here: 1. What will your audience see? 2. What will your viewers hear? 3. What are you trying to communicate or achieve?	**Media Resources** Students list all of the media they will need in order to construct this part of their digital story. This will help them later search for the right material. They will need to consider: 1. Music, songs, sound effects, voice recordings 2. Photo/video, images, diagrams 3. Text, titles, transitions, motion
Narration Students will write their accompanying narration here.		

Digital Storytelling Storyboarding Handout		
Digital Story Title		**Group Members**
Image	**Description**	**Media Resources**
Narration		

Prezi Presentation Preparation Resource Notes	
Prezi Title A title is chosen by students, and written here.	**Group Members** Student names are listed here.

Description

Students will answer one or all of the following questions here:

1. What are you trying to communicate?
2. What content will help support your message?
3. What structure or view path will your presentation contain, and in how many frames/slides?
4. What hook or imagery will you use to capture the audience at the start of the Prezi?

Media Resources

Students list all of the media that they will need for their presentation. This will help them later to search for the right material. They will need to consider:

1. Music, songs, voice recordings
2. Photo/video, images, diagrams, documents PowerPoints
3. Text, titles, animation effects

Prezi Canvas

Students can use this space to begin sketching a layout of the frames and the view path of their presentation.

Prezi Presentation Preparation Handout	
Prezi Title	**Group Members**
Description	
Media Resources	
Prezi Canvas	

Prezi Practice Exercise and Tutorial
Step One – Make your Prezi
To start out: • Select the 'My Prezis' Tab.   • Then, click 'Create a new Prezi'.
Step Two – Select a theme
Search for a template or make a selection from those presented, then click 'Use template', or click 'Start blank Prezi'. For example, search for a theme like 'sport'. For this exercise: • Click 'Start a blank Prezi'.
Step Three – The Prezi canvas
The top menu   Use the menu across the top of the screen to add a title, undo, redo, save, insert various media elements, customize aspects of the background or themes, to start presenting, share the Prezi, change the settings, or to exit the Prezi. For this exercise: • Click in the title section, and type the text 'Sports'.

Left side menu

Use the side menu on the left to add new frames, or change the type of frame to be added to the presentation canvas. There should be one frame on the Prezi presentation canvas already. So, for this example, add two more frames. These two additional frames can be any of the options available (e.g. bracket, circle, rectangle, or invisible). For this exercise:

- Select 'Circle'.
- Then, hover the mouse over the frame with a plus icon, click on it and drag the new frame to the Prezi canvas.
- Place the frame by letting go of the mouse. The frame can be moved around, and placed by clicking on it and using the hand icon.

The plus and minus buttons, or the transform icons can be used for resizing.

Right side menu

The side menu to the right can be used for various functions, including changing the zoom level or to show an overview of the entire presentation canvas. For this exercise:

- Click on the 'Plus' icon to zoom in.
- Then click on the 'Minus' icon to zoom out. Keep in mind that the mouse can also be used to zoom in and out.
- Finally, click on the 'House' icon to return to a zoom level that will show an overview of the entire Prezi.

Step Four – Inserting Text

To add text to the Prezi presentation canvas, click anywhere within the Prezi window, and begin typing. Text can be set as a title, subtitle, or body, and various font elements can be chosen such as font size and type, bulleting, and justification. For this exercise:

- Click near the top of the Prezi above the first frame, and type the word 'Sports'.
- Set the text as a title, and then place it appropriately.
- The text frame can be moved by clicking the hand icon, and resized using the plus and minus icons or by dragging the transform icons around the edge of the frame.
- The style of the frame can then be added as a favorite.

Step Five – Working with Content

Adding Content

From the top menu, select 'Insert'. A number of various types of content can then be inserted, including images from a file, symbols and shapes from a searchable index, YouTube videos, favorite items, a single frame or multi-frame layout, arrows, lines, highlights, background music from a file, a PDF, and a video or a PowerPoint from a file. For this exercise:

- Select 'Symbols & shapes', then in the search box type a search term or select an image like the bicycle.
- To select the bicycle image, click on it, then drag it to the Prezi canvas. The image can then be moved around by clicking the hand icon, and resized using the plus and minus icons or by dragging the transform icons around the edge of the frame surrounding the image.
- Options along the top of the image frame allow you to 'Crop' the image, 'favorite' the image, 'delete' the image, or 'replace' it.

Step Six – Working with Frames

Frame menu options

When a frame is selected, several menu options are available, including 'Zoom to frame', changing the 'Type' of frame, changing the color of the frame, adding the frame as a 'Favorite' or 'Delete'.

Grouping and Resizing with a frame

For this exercise:

- Move the image that you previously placed on the Prezi canvas to fit inside this new frame.
- After that, move the frame to any position that you like. You will notice that anything inside a frame will move with the frame.
- Click the frame to select it, and from the menu options, use the plus or minus buttons to change the size. You will notice that any content within the frame will also resize proportionally.

Adding animation to frames

To add animations to the content of a frame, right click on the frame, then select 'Animate frame contents'. For this exercise:

- 'Right click' on the frame with the image of the bicycle.
- Then, in the editing window, select the image and click on 'Add a fade in' effect.
- You can then preview the animation or click on 'Done' to return to the presentation canvas.

Step Seven – Editing the Viewing Path

Frame order

As you have been preparing your Prezi, you may have noticed that each frame has a number to the side of it. If the presentation is played as a slideshow, this number indicates when that particular frame will be shown. For this exercise:

- Click on the 'House' icon to see the entire presentation canvas. Note the numbers next to each frame showing their view order.

Changing frame order

When editing the frame viewing order, you will see that all the frame numbers are connected by a line to show the viewing path, and objects can be added between frames by dragging the plus icon of any of these lines to those objects. For this exercise:

- Click 'Edit path' found on the left side menu at the bottom to start work on changing the viewing order.

Setting the viewing order

The viewing order will be displayed on the left side menu by slide, and these slides can also be reordered. For this exercise:

- Click 'Clear all', under 'Edit path', and then click on the title text. This will then be labeled '1' and moved to the first slide position on the left menu.
- Next, click on each frame in the order that you would like to set them for presentation. The frames should now be labeled '2', '3', '4' respectively and added to the left slide menu. If desired, reorder the slides.
- Click 'Done' from the top menu.

Step Eight – Showing and Reviewing the Prezi

It is always a good idea to review your Prezi before it is exported or shared with a wider audience, and to make any necessary edits or adjustments as necessary. For this exercise:

- From the top menu, click 'Present'. This will then play the presentation in full screen mode, and you can move through the steps of the viewing path using the right or left arrows.
- Pressing 'esc' will exit the presentation mode and return you to editing.
- You can now work on improving the presentation.

Step Nine – Exporting and Sharing the Prezi

Once you have played back your Prezi, and are happy with the final review, you may choose to export it or to share it.

To export the Prezi

Click the 'Share' icon on the top menu, and select one of the following options:

- Click 'Download as PDF' to save the Prezi as a PDF file, with each frame or slide becoming a page.
- Click 'Download as portable Prezi' to obtain a zip file containing the presentation.

To share the Prezi

Click the 'Share' icon on the top menu, and select one of the options below:

- Click 'Share Prezi' to obtain a link to the Prezi, and be able to add people (by email address) who can view the Prezi. Options to set the privacy and duplication settings for the Prezi are also available here.
- Click 'Present remotely' to obtain a link that allows a maximum of thirty invited people to watch a remote presentation of the Prezi at the same time as you navigate and present.
- Click 'Share on Facebook' to obtain a link to email as well as the ability to share the Prezi on social media.

Prezi Presentation Tips
1. Start by mind mapping your presentation.
2. Use templates to help you get started.
3. Use 'Redo' or 'Undo' when editing.
4. Use magnifier buttons '+' or '-' to zoom in and out while you edit and present.
5. Use the highlighter to point out key information.
6. Zoom in on objects to give them focus.
7. Use the zoom tool sparingly.
8. Credit the sources that you use in your Prezi, including research and image-based resources.
9. Keep in mind that although Prezi auto-saves, you still need to click 'Save' and 'Exit' when you finish editing.
10. Stand to the left when presenting, as this will give your audience an anchor when reading the screen.

Podcast Design Plan Resource Notes	
Podcast Title A title is chosen by students, and written here.	**Group Members** Student names are listed here.
Guest(s) Potential guest(s) selected, and name(s) written here.	
Topic	What unit or lesson will be the focus?
Objectives	List the learning or interview objectives here.
Planning	What is the intent of the broadcast? How long will it go for? Will there be one long episode, or a series of shorter episodes? What style will the recording take? (e.g. audio or video) Where will the recording take place?
Producing	Appropriate hardware is required (e.g. microphone, webcam). Ensure that hardware is working, and students know how to use it. A production plan will need to be developed.
Publishing	Create an RSS feed to distribute your podcast, and provide access to show notes for listeners.
Promoting	Attempt to involve listeners: ask questions that will lead to comments being left (e.g. ask for future topic suggestions, or ask for questions to be left for you to answer in another episode); spread links to the episode; show notes or behind-the-scenes photos across social media.

Podcast Design Plan Handout		
Podcast Title	**Group Members**	
Guest(s) _____		
Topic	**Unit/Lesson** _____	
Objectives	1. _____ 2. _____	
Planning	Intent of broadcast _____ Length of broadcast _____ Number of episodes _____ Style of recording _____ Recording location _____	
Producing	Hardware required _____ _____ _____ ☐ Hardware is operational ☐ Hardware is usable ☐ Production plan developed*	
Publishing	☐ Files hosted ☐ RSS Feed created Show notes link _____ Transcript link _____	
Promoting	Listener involvement _____ _____ Links spread to _____ _____	

*Use the 'Podcast Production Plan Handout'.

Podcast Production Plan Resource Notes	
Introductory Music (30-60 seconds)	Play a unique identifier for your show that audience members can associate with you. This can then lead into the podcast, with the introduction monolog then spoken as a voiceover.
Introductory Monolog (30-60 seconds)	State who you are, introduce any guests, and state the topics to be discussed.
Topics (3-5 minutes each)	Stay focused on the key aspects of the topic by asking guests specific questions (or posing questions to yourself), and guiding guests back on track where necessary. It is advisable to prepare a script to follow for solo podcasts. Throughout each topic, remind the listeners that any resources or links will be posted as show notes, and where these can be obtained.
Closing Remarks (2 minutes)	Thank the audience for listening, thank any guests, mention the topic and/or guests of the next show, and remind the audience where to go for show notes.
Closing Music (2 minutes)	Play out the podcast with the same music as used in the introduction. This can be started during the closing remarks and continue afterwards.

Podcast Production Plan Handout	
Introductory Music (30-60 seconds)	
Introductory Monolog (30-60 seconds)	
Topic 1+ (3-5 minutes each)	
Closing Remarks (2 minutes)	
Closing Music (2 minutes)	

Screencast Design Plan Resource Notes	
Screencast Title A title is chosen by students, and written here.	**Group Members** Student names are listed here.

Application(s) Name the application(s) taking focus here.	
Topic	What unit or lesson will be covered?
Objectives	List the learning objectives of the screencast.
Format	Determine the format based on lesson objectives (e.g. demonstration, presentation, tutorial).
Scripting	Walk through the steps on screen that you intend to discuss; prepare an outline or script as you go. Read through the script for practice, and to determine the time required for recording.
Capturing	Decide on the area of the screen, or the applications, to be recorded. Recording can be conducted simultaneously with narration, or the voiceover can be added in postproduction.
Editing	Edit out mistakes; trim, add or sync the narration; add call-outs, zooms, and annotations.
Publishing	Publish the movie to a YouTube channel or learner management system (LMS), or distribute for in-class delivery. Provide access to program notes.
Promoting and Engaging	Promote the screencast on the class website for various stakeholders to see, and engage viewers by asking questions or asking them to comment.

Screencast Design Plan Handout	
Screencast Title	**Group Members**
Application(s) _____	

Topic	**Unit/Lesson** _____
Objectives	**1.** _____ **2.** _____
Format	**Type** _____
Scripting	**Time required** _____ ☐ **Production plan developed***
Capturing	**Area(s)/applications recorded** _____ **Hardware required** _____ ☐ **Hardware is operational** ☐ **Hardware is usable**
Editing	☐ **Narration synced** ☐ **Annotations, callouts, and zooms applied**
Publishing	**Screencast link** _____ **Program notes link** _____ **Transcript link** _____
Promoting and Engaging	**Links spread to** _____ **Viewer involvement** _____

*Use the 'Screencast Production Plan Handout'.

Screencast Production Plan	
Resource Notes	
Introduction **(30-60 seconds)**	Select the screen area that will become the focus, and provide a voiceover introduction to the topic or topics that will be discussed, with an overview of the steps involved.
Topics **(3-5 minutes each)**	Each topic-based section needs to stay on script. Keep the viewer informed, and tell them everything that you are doing. Zoom into and highlight features only when they are being discussed. Use annotations and callouts where necessary, and edit out any pauses or mistakes in post-production.
Closing Remarks **(2 minutes)**	Finish off by thanking the viewers and remind them of the topics covered and the knowledge and skills that have been imparted by watching the screencast, and how these skills can now be put to use.

Screencast Production Plan Handout	
Introduction (30-60 seconds)	
Topics (3-5 minutes each)	
Closing Remarks (2 minutes)	

Podcast/Screencast Summary and Review
Resource Notes

Podcast/Screencast Title	Group Members Student
A title is chosen by students, and written here.	names are listed here.

Summary Use sentence prompts to stimulate deep learning.

I learned Students identify and write at least one thing new that they learned from the podcast/screencast.

In particular I learned Students identify and write something new they learned that was surprising to them.

I really understood Students identify and write something new that they learned and understood very well.

I didn't really understand Students write something that they did not understand at all or need further clarification on.

This podcast/screencast has helped me better understand Students identify and write the objective of the screencast.

Review Questions (Use *Wh*-type questions to help promote surface learning – What? When? Where? Why? How?).

1. What … ? _____

_____

2. When … ? _____

_____

3. Where … ?_____

_____

4. Why … ? _____

_____

Podcast/Screencast Summary and Review Handout	
Podcast/Screencast Title	Group Members

Summary

I learned _____

_____

In particular I learned _____

_____

I really understood _____

_____

I didn't really understand _____

_____

This podcast/screencast has helped me better understand___

_____

Review Questions

1. _____

_____

2. _____

_____

3. _____

_____

4. _____

_____

Podcast/Screencast Show/Program Notes Resource Notes
Group members Write the name of groupe members here. **Image** Provide an image representative of your podcast, or an image of the guests interviewed (for podcasts) or an image representative of the application discussed (for screencasts). **Podcast/Screencast title** Write its name here. **Air date** Write the date of the broadcast here. **Guest(s)** Write the name(s) of guests here.
Podcast/Screencast overview Provide a short reminder of the topic of the podcast/screencast. Include a further tow or three sentences for: Podcasts – reminder of guest credentials, or your own if there were no guests. Screencasts – reminder of the importance of the applications(s) discussed.
Episode highlights Provide topic highlights using a hook, along with the time the topic is discussed. For example: *Dr Kent's tips to pass the TOEIC, and how you can master the exam easily.* [03:10].
Resources from this episode Provide links to all resources mentioned, and anything that you suggested as beneficial for viewers or listeners to follow up on. This might include: internet pages, journal articles, or any books, TV shows, and commercial products recommended.
Related articles Include links to places such as: an article (online or offline), a blog post, or a wiki page.

Podcast/Screencast Show/Program Notes Handout

Group members _____

Image

Podcast/Screencast title _____

Air date _____

Guest(s) _____

Podcast/Screencast overview

_____

_____

_____

Episode highlights

_____

_____

_____

_____

_____

Resources from this episode

_____

_____

_____

Related articles

_____

_____

_____

_____

7. Resources List

7. Resources List

As sites continuously go down, merge, and emerge, perhaps only a small selection of all appropriate resource content should be presented here. An attempt at keeping the number of resources to a select few for each type also provides a sample that is both comprehensive and extensive, but not overwhelming. Like any other instructor resource list, individuals will be able to add to the content as they find material that is useful, creating their own bookmark list, and over time, come to curate a vast resource library tailored to their individual teaching and learning context. Each section of this list is broken down into applications that are mostly all freely available for use with Android or iOS devices, computers, or web-based platforms.

Teachers who wish to make notes, or to record any additional resources that they come across, can use the notes section at the end of this chapter.

The following content is covered:
- App creation
- Audio creation/editing
- Blogs
- Bookmarking
- Books
- Coding
- Comic strip generators
- Copyright
- Digital story creation
- Image resources
- Image editing
- Interactive whiteboards
- Mashups
- Media timelines
- Music resources
- Podcasting
- Podcatchers
- Presentations
- Publishing
- QR codes
- Rubrics
- Screencasting
- Storyboarding and scripting
- Story creation apps
- Video editing
- Video resources
- WebQuests
- Wikis

App Creation

Android – n/a
iOS – n/a
Computer – n/a
Web

> *Android Creator* [free/paid] creates free Android apps without the need for programming knowledge.
>
> *AppMakr* [free/paid] is a template based application creator that relies on drag and drop of elements for the development of no-coding required applications. It is available in a variety of languages.
>
> *Appy Pie* [free/paid] relies on templates as well as drag and drop for users to begin creating their app. It requires no coding skills.
>
> *AppYourself* [paid] is an app creation tool aimed at the business market.
>
> *Como DIY* [paid] is a do-it-yourself app creation tool aimed to mostly target to businesses, and is available in a number of languages.
>
> *iBuildApp* [paid] is a template driven app creator for iPhone and Android phones.

Audio Creation/Editing

Android

> *PCM Recorder* [free] is a simple voice recorder.
>
> *Pocket WavePad* [free] records edits and adds effects to audio.
>
> *TapeMachine* [paid] is a graphical sound recorder and editor.

iOS

> *Pocket WavePad* [free] records edits and adds effects to audio.

Voice Memos [paid] is voice recorder that allows multitasking.

Computer

Audacity [free] is an open source digital editing program available for Mac and PC which you can use to record, edit and mix narration and music.

Pocket WavePad [free] records, edits, and adds effects to audio for Mac.

GoldWave [free/paid] is a digital audio editor that provides simple recording as well as more sophisticated processing, restoration, enhancement, and conversion for Windows and Linux. A free version is available for evaluation purposes, after which a lifetime license can be purchased.

Web

Twistedwave [free] is a browser-based audio editor that can record or edit any audio file.

Blogs

Android

Blogaway [free] is a simple application to allow blogging on-the-go. It works with Blogger and allows for post creation, adding of photos, videos, multiple account management, saving of drafts, bookmarking, and a host of formatting options.

iOS

Disqus [free] is a commenting system that can be included in blogs as an add-on. The application provides an easy way to moderate comments and publish responses to keep engagement levels high.

TravelPod – Travel Blog [free] is a blogging application that works on- and offline, and is designed to be used while traveling.

Computer – n/a

Web

Blogger.com [free] will host your blog for free, and aside from being very easy to use, it allows some level of privacy so it can be suitable for use as a class blogging site. From a single account, you can create as many blogs as you wish and determine who is allowed to comment on the content.

BuzzSumo [paid] allows users to search for blog posts that have been highly shared across social media.

Edublogs.org [free] allows teachers to create and mange their own and students' websites. There is room for customization of design and the ability to add various media to this private and secure platform.

Kidblog.org [free] is an easy-to-use, safe, and secure publishing platform designed for students in grades K-12. There are a number of excellent features including privacy and password protection, and there is no need for student personal information to be collected, nor is there any advertising. It is free for up to fifty students per class.

WordPress.org [free] is one of the most popular blogging platforms in use today as it is open- source and is easily customizable. The downloadable software for self-hosting purposes is much more flexible than that available on the blogging platform.

Twitter [free] deserves a mention here as it is useful for microblogging (posting short frequent updates). It allows users to post and read short 140-character posts called 'tweets'.

Tumblr [free] is a blogging platform open to those over thirteen years of age, with most users using pen names over their real names when blogging. Users can post on their blog, follow others, and search posts. It is unique in that posts are divided into media types: text, photo, quote, link, chat, audio, and video.

Bookmarking

Android

Bookmark [free] is a cross-platform app that allows for the syncing of bookmarks across different browsers and devices.

Delicious [free] provides users with the ability to organize links to content on the internet that they would like to save, the ability to discover links, edit tags and comments, and also to explore content saved by friends.

Facebook Save [free] is a built-in option for saving Facebook news content to read at a later date.

Instapaper [free] provides an offline archiving solution for web pages, and it presents this content to be read in newspaper fashion. Content can be highlighted, and notes can be added while reading.

Pinterest [free] allows users to pin posts (for example, web pages, images, and videos) and organize them around a common theme.

Pocket [free] integrates with a large number of third party applications that allow for the building of bookmarks. Web pages, videos, images, and whatever else can be used offline for bookmarking. Archiving maintains the links but removes the content from offline availability.

iOS

Delicious [free] allows users to save content from the internet (including web pages, blog posts, tweets, pictures, and video), and provides options for searching through others' collections of links.

Facebook Save [free] is a built-in option for saving Facebook news content to read at a later date.

Instapaper [free] provides an offline archiving solution for web pages and presents this content to be read in newspaper fashion. Content can be highlighted, and notes can be added while reading.

Pinterest [free] allows users to pin posts (for example, web pages, images, and videos) and organize them around a common theme.

Pocket [free] integrates with a large number of third party applications that allow for the building of bookmarks. Web pages, videos, images, and whatever else can be used offline for bookmarking. Archiving maintains the links but removes the content from offline availability.

Computer

EdwinSoft's UltimateDemon [paid] is link building software that helps to provide search engine optimization to a website.

Pinterest [free] allows users to pin posts (for example, web pages, images, and videos) and organize them around a common theme.

Pocket [free] integrates with a large number of third party applications that allow for the building of bookmarks. Web pages, videos, images, and whatever else can be used offline for bookmarking. Archiving maintains the links but removes the content from offline availability.

ReadKit [trial/paid] offers an Apple Mac curative and archiving platform for the content found in your other bookmarking applications (like Pocket and Instapaper) and RSS readers, and provides an extra level of organization to this content.

Web

Delicious [free] is a social bookmarking site that allows users to bookmark webpages to the internet instead of locally.

Facebook Save [free] is a built-in option for saving Facebook news content to read at a later date.

Instapaper [free] provides an offline archiving solution for web pages, and it presents this content to be read in newspaper fashion. Content can be highlighted, and notes can be added while reading.

OnlyWire [paid] works with WordPress and offers automatic submission of content to social networking and social bookmarking sites.

Pocket [free] integrates with a large number of third party applications that allow for the building of bookmarks. Web pages, videos, images, and whatever else can be used offline for bookmarking. Archiving maintains the links but removes the content from offline availability.

Books

Android
  Wattpad Free Books [free] provides access to free stories and books written by aspiring authors.
iOS
  Free Books – Ultimate Classics Library [free] features free access to 23,469 classic books.
Computer – n/a
Web
  BookRix [free] allows access to thousands of books to read either online or to download as ebooks.
  Children's Storybooks Online [free] provides a series of illustrated stories for all ages to read.

Coding

Android
  Run Marco! [free] offers users the opportunity to play an adventure game while they learn to code. The application presents instructions using 'Blocky', which is the same as that used by the official Hour of Code tutorials.
  Tynker [free] is an easy way for children to learn programming skills as they solve puzzles to learn concepts

and build games, or control robots and drones. A number of templates are available for free.

iOS

Codea [paid] is a software development tool that uses the Lua programming language to teach users how to program.

Hopscotch [free] is an application that allows users to begin learning to code by making games similar to Angry Birds, and sharing them so others can play them.

ScratchJr [free] allows users to program their own interactive stories and games by snapping together graphical programming blocks. The application was inspired by the Scratch programming language.

Tynker [free] is an easy way for children to learn programming skills as they solve puzzles to learn concepts and build games, or control robots and drones. A number of templates are available for free.

Computer

Scratch [free] allows users to create stories, games, and animations using the Scratch programming language, and then share these with others. It is a project of the Lifelong Kindergarten Group at the MIT Media Lab.

Lightbot – Programming Puzzles [paid] is an OS X game-based application that allows players to use programming logic to solve levels. The app is also available for Android and iOS devices.

Web – n/a

Comic Strip Generators

Android

Comic Maker [free] creates comics from the photo gallery.

Comic Strip It! Lite [free] takes photos or use photo gallery images to create a comic.

iOS

Comic Life 3 [paid] turns photos into comic pages, or creates an entire comic from scratch using templates to build pages with speech balloons, comic lettering, and photo filters.

ToonTastic [free] is a wizard-based animated comic or cartoon creator.

Strip Designer [paid] is software for comic creation that uses camera, library, or Facebook photo options to create a comic.

Computer

Comic Creator [paid] is a basic template driven comic creator for use on a Windows computer.

Web

Pixton [free/paid] is an easy to use comprehensive online comic creator that supports narration, and offers a range of signup options from a free fun option to paid educator/business accounts.

MakeBeliefsComix [free] is a basic comic creator that uses black and white images over a four-panel comic strip. An iOS version is also available.

Toonlet [free] allows for anyone to create their own cartoon characters and web comics.

Toondoo [free] allows for the drag and drop creation of comic strips. An iOS version is also available.

Copyright

Android – n/a
iOS – n/a
Computer – n/a
Web

Creative Commons Licenses [free] gives detailed information regarding the various types of licensing afforded to creative commons, and the permissions that each license grants for the use specific works.

Image Codr [free] can assist learners and teachers alike in determining how a Flickr image can be used (as determined by the original photographer), and provides users with an automatically generated Creative Commons citation regarding the images use within digital projects.

Digital Story Creation

Android
Com-Phone Story Maker [free] combines audio, photos, and text to create stories while allowing for three different layers of audio.

WeVideo [free] is a web-based video editor that can mix images, text, video, and audio.

iOS
30hands [free] creates a story by adding narration to photos.

Magisto [free] uses a wizard to create a short video based on provided images or video content.

Splice [free/paid] combines photos, videos, music and narrations. Effects and transitions can be added.

WeVideo [free] is a web-based video editor that can mix images, text, video, and audio.

Computer
iMovie [paid] provides video creation and editing software that can create easily shareable content on a Mac. An iOS version is available.

Microsoft Photo Story 3 [free] for Windows lets you create slideshows from a wizard that includes audio, narration, and images.

Windows Movie Maker [free] for Windows operating systems is a video editing software application that allows for narration, audio, images, and video to be mixed and edited, and it comes with transitions and special effects.

Web
Animoto [paid] allows users to submit songs, choose a theme, add their photos, videos, and text to create a digital story that they can share.

Meograph [free] is a digital storytelling tool that relies on Google Earth to create map-based and timeline-based narrated stories.

WeVideo [free] is a web-based video editor that can mix images, text, video, and audio.

Image Resources

Android – n/a
iOS – n/a
Computer – n/a
Web

Cagle Cartoons [free] provides access to a number of political cartoons from around the world. The images are organized by topic with artists categorized by country.

Flickr Creative Commons [free] provides images that can be used for almost any educational project, as long as proper citation is followed

FreeFoto.com [free] has a photos area that is available under three licensing options: recognition, Creative Commons, and commercial.

Morguefile [free] provides a range of images that are copyright free, and are available for use with few or no restrictions.

Pics4Learning.com [free] is a website that provides safe and free images for educational uses. Images here are copyright-friendly and can be used for classrooms, multimedia projects, websites, videos, portfolios, or other projects.

PicSearch [free] allows you to search the internet for images, but be aware that the image may not be copyright-free, or that it may require permission to be used in projects or in any other educational contexts.

The Library of Congress Prints & Photographs Online Catalog [free] makes an attempt to ensure that as many of their images as possible are available online in a digital format.

Wikimedia [free] serves as a point from where all the images and video posted in Wikipedia can be viewed. Most of the images found here are either copyright-free or free for use with minimal restrictions.

Image Editing

Android

PicSay [free] can edit photos, overlay titles, and add special effects.

FX Camera [free] is a photo booth app that allows users to add various effects to photographs.

iOS

PhotoPad [free] can create, edit, and save vector illustrations. It can also work with photo library images.

ScreenChomp [free] allows you to share, explain, and markup images.

Computer

PhotoPad [paid] is an image editor for OS X.

PaintShop Pro [paid] is a comprehensive image editing package for Windows.

Web

Adobe Photoshop CC [paid] is a comprehensive cloud-based image editing package.

Phixr [free] is an online photo editor with various filters and effects, and it can connect to various social media sites.

FotoFlexer [free] is an online image editor offering a number of effects, distortions, and other features.

Pixlr [paid] is a comprehensive online photo editing app.

Interactive Whiteboards

Android

ExplainEverything [free] allows users to share their content by using an interactive screencasting whiteboard.

Interactive Whiteboard [free] is a virtual whiteboard that can be used for drawing or teaching various concepts as it allows for multiple finger input, straight line drawing mode, drawing move mode, and various other features.

PPT and Whiteboard Sharing [free] provides a way to share presentations, videos, and drawings in various settings including the classroom, the boardroom, and online meetings.

Whiteboard: Collaborative Draw [free] is a collaborative drawing application that allows real-time painting.

iOS

Doceri [trial/paid] combines screencasting, desktop control, and an interactive whiteboard in one application, with control through Airplay or through Mac or PC.

Educreations Interactive Whiteboard [free] is an interactive whiteboard and screencasting tool that allows annotation, animation, and narration of a number of content types.

Screenchomp [free] allows users to annotate pictures or to use the application as a whiteboard. Any work completed with the application can be saved automatically to the internet.

ShowMe Interactive Whiteboard [free] allows voice-over recording of whiteboard interactions so that tutorials can be created easily before being shared online.

Computer

Open Sakore [free] is open-source and it is dedicated to teacher and student use. It allows for insertion of multiple document types, along with annotation capabilities for commenting drawing and highlighting content.

Smoothboard Air [free] is a collaborative interactive whiteboard for multiple iPads and for Android tablets. It allows users to annotate desktop applications wirelessly through the use of a web browser.

Web

A Web Whiteboard [free] is a online whiteboard application that allows a number of devices (like computers, tablets, and smartphones), to draw sketches, and to collaborate with others around the globe.

Realtime Board [free] is a whiteboard in a browser that allows for collaboration among a number of users.

Twiddla [free] is a web-based meeting environment that allows users to mark up photos, graphics, and websites, or to just start out with a blank canvas.

Web Whiteboard [free] is a simple way to draw and write together online by creating an online whiteboard with a click, and sharing it live or by sending the link to others.

Mashups

Android

Edjing 5 DJ Music Mixer [free] not only transforms any android device into a turntable, but it provides access to a range of music libraries.

iOS

iMashup [paid] is a professional quality remixing app that allows users to create their own mashups and remixes.

Pacemaker [free] allows users to create and save mixes on an iPhone or iWatch, and to DJ live from iPad devices.

Computer

Mixxx [free] is an advanced open source DJ package that includes an extensive array of features for OS X and Windows.

Web

Mashstix [free] is a website with user submitted mashups available.

Media Timelines

Android

RWT Timelines [free] allows students to create a graphical representation of any event or process by displaying items sequentially along a line. The final product can be exported as a pdf, or saved to the device's camera roll.

Timeline [free] allows users to create timelines and associate them with colors, and to view multiple timelines together. It is a useful reference tool for remembering dates.

iOS

TimelineBuilder [paid] allows users to create custom timelines with images and text with unique beginning and end dates.

Timeline Maker [free] provides an easy way to display a series of events in a chronological order.

Computer

Edraw Timeline Maker [paid] is a tool that makes it simple to create a professional looking timeline, history, schedule, time table, or project plan diagram from scratch.

TimelineMaker [paid] provides a simplified timeline charting tool aimed at project planners, and business professionals, and those in educational contexts.

Web

Capzles [free] allows users to create rich multimedia experiences from videos, photos, music, blogs, and documents by integrating these into a timeline of sequential events, and then share them on various social media platforms.

Hstry [free] is specifically designed for the education sector, and it allows teachers and students to create interactive timelines for assignments and online sharing.

OurStory [free] offers a means for creating story-based timelines with pictures.

Timeline [free] from *readwritethink* allows students of all ages to easily create a graphical representation of related items or events in sequential order and display them along a line using various images and text.

TimeGlider [free] is a web-based timeline project creator that allows zooming and panning across timelines. Users are able to set the size of events as they relate to importance.

Tiki-Toki [free/paid] is a web-based timeline editor that allows viewing of timelines in 3D, and it allows for the integration of images and videos.

WhenInTime [free] is a web application for creating and sharing media-based timelines.

Music Resources

Android

FindSounds [free] can be used to search the internet for sounds that can then be saved as ringtones, notifications, or alarms.

Shazam [free] allows Android device users to identify the music playing around them, as well as discover song lyrics, and other music related information and tracks.

iOS

Shazam [free] allows iOS device users to identify the music playing around them, as well as discover song lyrics, and other music related information and tracks.

Computer – n/a

Web

300 Monks [free] provides a comprehensive source of royalty free music.

ccMixter [free] is a free music site that is community based and promotes a remix culture. *A cappella* and remix tracks licensed under Creative Commons are available for download and use in creative works.

FMA (Free Music Archive) [free] provides access to a range of free music based on a wide variety of genre. The music is offered free under various licenses for use.

Find Sounds [free] is a long-running service that can be used to search the internet for various sounds that can then be incorporated into various projects.

FreePlay Music [free] is a service that searches the internet for free music that can be used in YouTube videos and other projects.

Podcasting

Android

Podomatic Podcast & Mix Player [free] provides access to a wide variety of podcasts, listening in offline mode, and features such as a dynamic social feed so you can see the podcasts Facebook friends follow and like.

iOS

PodOmatic Podcast Player [free] provides access to a wide variety of podcasts, listening in offline mode, and features such as a dynamic social feed so you can see the podcasts Facebook friends follow and like.

Computer

Audacity [free] is a free multi-track audio recorder and editor with some very powerful features that include those for adding effects to files and conducting analysis of the audio recorded.

iTunes [free] offers media on demand and a way to organize and enjoy music, movies, and TV shows, as well as accessing and subscribing to podcasts and screencasts.

LoudBlog [free] is a Content Management System (CMS) for podcasts. This program automatically generates skinnable websites and RSS-feeds for audio and video podcasts, including provision for show notes and links.

PodcastGenerator [free] is an open source content management system for podcast publishing. It provides a comprehensive range of tools to manage all aspects of podcast publishing.

PodProducer [free] allows for the recording of voice and the adding of effects.

Web

ESLPod [free] provides a range of podcast content tailored to second-language learners of English from specific topics through to test-taking guides.

FeedForAll [free] allows for the creation, editing, and publishing of RSS feeds.

Feedity [free] is an online tool for creating an RSS feed for any web page, with an option to upgrade to a premium account that offers additional features.

FETCHRSS: RSS Generator [free] is an online RSS feed generator, that can create a feed out of almost any web page, automatically updates the RSS feed when new content is added to the web page, and generates an RSS for a social networking site.

OPML Viewer [free] allows users to view the contents of outline processor markup language (OPML) files.

Podcast Alley [free] is the place to go if you are interested in podcasts, want to gain access to the top podcasts, and want to find out the latest news about podcasts.

Pod Gallery [free] is a podcasting website where podcasters can share their episodes, and where listeners can subscribe.

QT-ESL Podcasts [free] provides a range of podcasts that cover oral grammar practice and includes scripts and worksheets.

SoundCloud [free] is a social sound platform where anyone is able to create and share audio.

Podcatchers

Android

Podcast Player [free] provides a range of podcast discovery options and tools, along with a range of features including a sleep timer, video support, intelligent silence skip and volume boost, as well as support for tablet, Chromecast, and Android Wear.

Podcast Republic [free] is an application that is ad-supported. It offers a variety of features from podcast discovery and automatic downloading through to storage management, sleep timer, and car mode. Support is also included from Chromecast and Android Wear.

Pocket Casts [paid] shows subscribed podcasts in a tile format, with easy sorting and categorization functions. Video podcast is also supported, along with auto-download and cleanup of downloaded and played episodes to save on storage space. Several features allow it to stand out, including a sleep timer as well as its cross-platform nature that grants it the ability to sync between multiple devices and mobile operating systems.

iOS

Overcast: Podcast Player [free] provides a combination of powerful audio and podcast management features. The application comes with a wide variety of features that allow it to download episodes, send notifications of new episodes, and play content offline or by streaming. It can also normalize speech levels, and speed through gaps and silence in podcasts.

Castro: High Fidelty Podcasts [free] is a simple and easy to use podcatcher. It provides a simple design with automatic episode download, dynamic storage management, along with episode streaming.

Pocket Casts [paid] shows subscribed podcasts in a tile format, with easy sorting and categorization functions. Video podcast is also supported, along with auto-download and cleanup of downloaded and played episodes to save on storage space. Several features allow it to stand out, including a sleep timer as well as its cross-platform nature that grants it the ability to sync between multiple devices and mobile operating systems.

Computer

gPodder [free] is an open source media aggregator and podcast client. It is able to store information in the cloud on which shows you have listened to, and it allows for the local installation of the client for download of content.

iTunes [free] is a comprehensive media aggregator that provides comprehensive support for media management, the audio and video playback of local media, podcast search and subscription, along with automatic downloads, syncing and streaming, and many other features.

Juice [free] is a long-standing cross platform no-frills podcast aggregator that is open source, and specifically designed to manage podcasts. Features include auto cleanup, centralized feed management, and for Windows users, accessibility options for the blind and visually impaired.

Web

Cloud Caster [free] is a web-based podcaster which works across all mobile devices. It syncs progress and playlists across platforms, and provides search and support for audio and video podcasts.

Presentations

Android

Glogster [free] allows students using an Android-based device to create online multimedia posters, or Glogs, from a combination of media types (from audio, graphic, to video), and hyperlinks.

Google Slides [free] allows Android device users with a Google account a means of creating, editing, and collaborating with others on presentations.

LinkedIn SlideShare [free] allows Android device users the ability to search and explore for a variety of presentations, infographics, and documents on topics of their interest.

Microsoft PowerPoint [free] allows users to view PowerPoint presentations on their device for free, and to make edits and changes on the go.

iOS

Glogster [free] allows students using an iOS device to create online multimedia posters, or Glogs, from a combination of media types (from audio, graphic, to video), and hyperlinks.

Google Slides [free] allows iOS device users with a Google account a means of creating, editing, and collaborating with others on presentations.

Keynote [free] is a powerful presentation app that allows users to develop comprehensive presentations with animations, transitions, and multimedia elements.

LinkedIn SlideShare [free] allows iOS device users the ability to search and explore for a variety of presentations, infographics, and documents on topics of their interest.

Microsoft PowerPoint [free] allows users to view PowerPoint presentations on their device for free, and to make edits and changes on the go.

Computer

Microsoft PowerPoint [paid] is a comprehensive presentation software application, and is perhaps the most used and recognizable.

Keynote [free] is a powerful presentation app that allows users to develop comprehensive presentations with animations, transitions, and multimedia elements.

Web

Bunkr [free] is a presentation tool that displays any online content including social media posts, images, videos, audio, articles, and files.

Glogster [free] allows students to create online multimedia posters, or Glogs, from a combination of media types (from audio, graphic, to video), and hyperlinks.

Google Slides [free] allows those with a Google account, a means of creating, editing, and collaborating with others on presentations.

LinkedIn SlideShare [free] allows users to search for presentations, infographics, documents and other items on topics of their interest.

Microsoft PowerPoint Online [free] extends the Microsoft PowerPoint experience to the web browser with OneDrive integration, and allows users to create, edit, and view files on the go.

Prezi [free] is a visually oriented presentation packaged that also allows users to upload PowerPoint slides, and customize them, or use a variety of their own images, text, audio, and video.

Slidebean [free] offers a one-click presentation development system that incorporates a variety of templates into the design of presentations.

Slides [free] is a place for creating, presenting, and sharing slide decks.

Swipe [free] allows users to share a presentation link with anyone across any device, and it allows viewers to interact with the presentation on several levels, from collaboration through to taking polls.

VoiceThread [free] allows users to import various media such as images, PowerPoints, and PDFs. It provides a means of making audio or video recordings concerning those media artifacts, and it also allows other users to reply to the initial comments, by audio or video means, as the presentation progresses.

Publishing

Android

Book Creator Free [free] offers a simple means of creating a variety of ebooks including picture books, comic and photo books, and journals and textbooks. It allows for the use of images, narration, texts, annotations and drawings.

Book Writer Free [free] is a simple book creation application that allows users to share their content with others.

My Story Builder [free] is a simple, 'suitable for children', book editor.

Scribble: Kids Book Maker [paid] is an application that allows children to write, illustrate, and publish their own comprehensive stories in a range of formations including video export. It contains a series of story starters, stickers, and backgrounds to help them work on creating stories from the start.

iOS

Book Creator Free [free] offers a simple means of creating a variety of ebooks including picture books, comic and photo books, and journals and textbooks. It allows for the use of images, narration, texts, annotations and drawings.

Creative Book Builder [paid] is a professional ebook editor and generator which can also extend the utility of ebooks through the use of a range of widgets.

Demibooks Composer Pro [free] builds interactive books with animation, audio, images, and effects.

Scribble Press – Creative Book Maker for Kids [paid] contains a series of story starters, stickers and backgrounds to help get young kids working on creating stories that can be turned into ebooks.

Computer

Android Book App Maker [paid] provides users with the ability to turn content into a flip-book app.

iBooks Author [free] provides a series of templates and styles to assist in the development of ebooks for the iBook store.

Kotobee [free] provides free software to assist in the creation of ebooks and libraries for a range of platforms.

Web

Blurb [paid] is just one of many online services that can assist in the creation of ebooks.

QR Codes

Android

I-nigma QR & Barcode Scanner (free) is a versatile barcode and QR code reader that can scan a multitude of codes and share these codes as well.

QR Code Reader (free) is a simple QR Code and product barcode scanner.

QR Droid Code Scanner (free) is a powerful barcode, QR code, and Data Matrix scanner that offers multi-language support.

iOS

Bakodo – Barcode Scanner and QR Barcode Reader (free) scans all types of QR codes and barcodes.

QR Reader for iPhone (free) scans a variety of codes including QR codes and barcodes, and features auto-detect scanning.

QRafter – QR Code and Barcode Reader and Generator (free) is a two-dimensional barcode scanner for iOS. Along with a variety of useful features, it can scan and generate QR codes.

Computer

CodeTwo QR Code Desktop Reader (free) allows users to scan QR codes directly from their screen onto their desktop. Users select the QR code to be read by selecting the area with a QR code using their mouse.

QR-Code Studio (free) is for Mac and Windows computers. The QR code maker software is freeware.

Web

QR Code Generator (free) creates QR codes, in a limited number of formats, for free.

QR Stuff QR Code Generator (free) creates QR codes from a various types of data such as website URLs, image files, PDF files, and so on, with static and dynamic embedding options.

The QR Code Generator (free) allows for the free scan and generation of QR codes for a variety of uses.

Rubrics

Android

Daily Rubric: Any Curriculum [free] allows teachers to create and use rubrics from their Android device. Rubrics can be designed from curriculum outcomes, or based on the pre-loaded Common Core Standards.

iOS

Easy Assessment [paid] offers a means to capture and assess performance based on custom created rubrics, scale, or criteria.

Rubrics [paid] allows instructors to track student performance and produce reports based on custom rubrics and grading options.

Computer – n/a

Web

Kathy Shrock's Guide to Everything: Assessment and Rubrics [free] provides access to a wide range of rubrics to help guide assessment of students.

iRubric [free] is a website where instructors can create their own rubrics, or they can build off those made available from other instructors.

RubiStar [free] allows instructors to create their own rubrics using templates designed for core subjects as well as art, music, and multimedia.

Screencasting

Android

AZ Screen Recorder [free] is a screen recording application that offers several features, including the ability to capture the front camera as well as screen recording. It also provides video trimming.

ilos Screen Recorder [free] is a simple application that records the screen and provides audio capture as well.

Telecine [free] is an open source application that allows screen recording through the use of overlays.

iOS

Doceri [trial/paid] combines screencasting, desktop control, and an interactive whiteboard in one application, with control through Airplay or through Mac or PC.

Educreations Interactive Whiteboard [free] is an interactive whiteboard and screencasting tool that allows annotation, animation, and narration of a number of content types.

Screenchomp [free] allows users to annotate pictures or to use the application as a whiteboard. Any work completed with the application can be saved automatically to the internet.

Computer

ilos screen recorder [free] automatically uploads content to their servers for storage and playback.

Screencast-O-Matic [free] offers fifteen minutes of recording time for free, both for screen and webcam, and allows users to save to places such as YouTube or as a video file.

TechSmith Camtasia Studio [free trial] is a comprehensive screen recording application that allows for audio and webcam capture as well as highlighting, adding media, and editing of recordings.

Web – n/a

Storyboarding and Scripting

Android

Ray Story Board [free] is a simple storyboard creator that lets users build storyboards from photos or gallery images, create multiple storyboards, and animate them using a slideshow feature.

Storyboard Studio [paid] is a mobile storyboarding writing tool that is suitable for artists and non-artists alike.

iOS

Penultimate [free] provides a natural feel of writing and sketching on paper, and connects to Evernote.

Storyboard Composer [paid] is a mobile storyboard previsualiztion composer for animators, art directors, film students, film directors, or anyone who would like to visualize their story.

Computer

FrameForge Previz Studio [paid] allows users to develop and previsualize films, TV shows, commercials, or similar projects at a professional level.

Storyboardpro [paid] is professional level software that combines drawing and animation tools with camera controls.

StoryBoard Quick Studio [paid] allows for the fast creation of storyboards with QuickShots, has a print-to-sketch feature, and comes with a series of character poses for integration into storylines.

Web

Google Docs [free] can be used, along with any note-taking or document editor, as a make-shift storyboard by integrating photos or pictures into the document to outline a process or the actions for a story. It is also available as an Android and iOS app.

StoryboardThat [free trial] offers an edition that allows educators to build diagrams, and visualize workflow. It features a drag and drop interface and an extensive image library.

Story Creation Apps

Android

StoryMaker 1 [free] provides a means of creating stories using templates and overlays, and the possibility of using audio, photos, or video.

Storehouse [free] allows users to share a collection of photos in a collage or album, or by telling a story that links the photos.

iOS

StoryKit [free] allows for the creation of an electronic storybook through the use of images, simple drawings, recording of sound, and by the addition of text.

Storyrobe [paid] makes photo-based slideshows with voice recording.

FotoBabble [free] adds audio to a photo to make a talking postcard.

Sock Puppets [free] lets users create lip-synced videos with characters. Various puppets, props, scenery, and backgrounds can be used.

Computer

Cartoon Story Maker 1.1 [free] is a simple program that creates 2D cartoon stories with conversations, dialogs (recorded and/or speech bubble), and various backgrounds.

StoryMaker [free/trial] is game-based software that asks for parts of speech (such as nouns, verbs, adjectives), and these are then inserted into a story with sometimes comical results. Educators can edit and customize aspects of the aspects of the program for their context. Backgrounds can be imported, but character templates are built in.

Web

Littlebirdtales [free] provides younger learners the ability to create digital storybooks.

Pixton [free/paid] is a visual writing tool that allows users to make a comic using images, clipart backgrounds and artwork, as well as speech bubbles.

Storynet.org [free] is a website that aims at connecting people to and through storytelling.

StoryJumper [free] allows users to create illustrated storybooks from scratch or from existing templates.

Video Editing

Android

VideoShow – Video Editor [free] is an all-in-one video editor and slideshow producer that provides music, themes, filters, emojis, as well as text input.

VidTrim [free] is a video editor and organizer that allows the trimming, editing, and saving of videos.

VivaVideo: Free Video Editor [free] is a comprehensive video editor and movie maker that facilitates the creation of video-based stories.

WeVideo [free] is a comprehensive and easy to use video editor that can mix images, text, video, and audio.

iOS

iMovie [paid] is video creation and editing software that can create easily shareable content.

Splice [free] is a video editor that adds music and effects to images and videos with narration. It includes access to free songs, sound effects, text overlays, transitions, filters, and various editing tools.

ReelDirector II [paid] is a full-featured video editing app.

WeVideo [free] is an easy to use and comprehensive video editor that can mix audio, images, text, and audio.

Computer

Windows Movie Maker [free] is a video editing software application that allows for narration, audio, images, and video to be mixed and edited with transitions and special effects.

Web

Video Toolbox [free] is an online video editing and conversion tool.

WeVideo [free] is a comprehensive and easy to use web-based video editor that can mix images, text, video, and audio together to form a compelling story.

Video Resources

Android

TED [free] provides more than 2,000 TED talks from various people by topic and mood, and on a variety of topics.

Vimeo [free] is a variety of videos are available across a wide variety of topics and genres, with users having the ability to upload their own content as well.

YouTube [free] allows for editing and uploading of videos, where one can subscribe to various channels that offer a wide variety of videos on various topics and genres.

iOS

TED [free] provides more than 2,000 TED talks from various people by topic and mood, and on a variety of topics.

Vimeo [free] provides a variety of videos which are available across a wide variety of topics and genres. Users are able to upload their own content as well.

YouTube [free] allows for editing and uploading of videos, where once can subscribe to various channels that offer a wide variety of videos on various topics and genres.

Computer – n/a

Web

Clipcanvas [free] allows for the download of 600,000 royalty free HD and 4K video and film clips.

Mazwai [free] maintains a collection of free to use HD video clips and footage, and some unique time-lapse and slow motion video footages that are provided under the Creative Commons Attribution license if used commercially.

Motion Backgrounds for Free [free] is a place to download professional quality motion backgrounds and video footage.

Motion Elements [free] is a good source for premium stock videos, offering around 400 videos for free, as well as free After Effects templates.

Neo's Clip Archive [free] offers nearly 3,500 free video clips sorted by 25 categories free for use for personal, non-commercial purposes.

Pexels Videos [free] brings under one roof a video library of Creative Commons Zero licensed stock videos from a variety of different sources.

SaveTube [free] allows users to rip YouTube videos to their local computer in various audio or video-based formats.

Savevideo.me [free] allows users to rip videos from a variety of sites to their local computer.

TeacherTube [free] is an online resource that helps users to view and share videos, photos, audio, and documents on almost any topic.

WebQuests

Android – n/a
iOS – n/a
Computer – n/a
Web

Building a WebQuest [free] is a comprehensive overview of the template to follow when there is a need to construct a WebQuest.

Having Fun with Reading [free] is a WebQuest for college and adult level learners of English, where learners interact with texts and complete activities that promote cooperative and collaborative learning along with reading narrative comprehension skills.

Idioms in Your Pocket [free] is a WebQuest that is designed for high school and adult ESL students, and it allows them to discover the various meanings of English idioms.

OneStopEnglish WebQuests [free] provides a selection of WebQuests covering major holidays.

Pre-Writing Your WebQuest [free] provides prompts for users to complete in order to develop a WebQuest.

QuestGarden [free/paid] is a site designed by Bernie Dodge, the creator of WebQuests, for use by pre- and in-service teachers, professional developers, other educators, and those who work with them. The site provides hosting and template creation of WebQuests that then become searchable.

Using WebQuests to Teach English [free] is a WebQuest that can be used to teach teachers about WebQuests.

WebQuestDirect [free] is described as the world's largest searchable directory of WebQuest reviews.

WebQuest.Org [free] provides comprehensive information pertaining to the WebQuest model, and is run by Bernie Dodge, the creator of WebQuests.

Zunal [free/paid] is a site for educators to create, host, and then share their WebQuests with others.

Wikis

Android

EveryWiki: Wikipedia++ [free] aims to provide access to many wikis from a central application.

wikiHow [free] is the application associated with the leading how-to-guide wikiHow. It allows for searching of the wiki to find step-by-step instructions on how to complete almost any task.

iOS

Hack My Life – Life Hack Wiki [free] is an application that seeks to provide access to all possible life hacks. A life hack is a strategy or technique that can be used or adopted to allow for better time management or for getting more out of everyday activities.

Lyrically [free] offers access to a list of song lyrics curated by fans. Searches can be undertaken by track, artist, or by song, and there is support for in-app purchases.

Computer

DokuWiki [free] is a PHP based highly customizable and fully extensible wiki software platform. The advantage is that it requires no databases as all the data is stored in plain text, and for this reason, it is very popular and used by many sites. It has a variety of useful features, from locking to avoid edits through to a spam blacklist.

MediaWiki [free] is open-source and it is the wiki software used by Wikipedia. It is available in a number of languages, released under a general public license (GPL), and written in PHP: Hypertext Preprocessor (PHP) a server-side scripting language. There are many extensions and plugins available for free, including a what-you-see-is-what-you-get (WYSIWYG) editor.

Web

PBworks [free] (formerly PBwiki) is a real-time collaborative editing system with several solutions including one for educators. It offers a single workspace, where student accounts can be created without email addresses, and easy editing without the need for coding.

PmWiki [free] is a wiki tool that gives user-access control over individual pages, so they can be set for access by specific people with it being possible to set different passwords for each page.

The software also allows for navigation trails through individual sections, insertion of tables, and provides a printable layout.

Wikidot [free] offers members the ability to create a wiki-based website with forums, where they can create a community, or publish and share documents and content.

Wikispaces [free] is a wiki hosting service that provides educators with a means to monitor student progress in real time and the ability to easily create projects and assign them to students, as well as editing tools and a social newsfeed.

Teacher Notes

Android

iOS

Computer

Web

References

Ali, A. D. (2016). Effectiveness of Using Screencast Feedback on EFL Students' Writing and Perception. *English Language Teaching, 9*(8), 106-121.

Aljehani, W. M. A. (2015). Using Prezi presentation software to enhance vocabulary learning of EFL secondary school students. *Educational Research International, 4*(4). 67-81.

Assink, M. (2006). Inhibitors of disruptive innovation capability: A conceptual model. *European Journal of Innovation Management, 9*(2), 215-233.

Bell, T., Cockburn, A., Wingkvist, A., & Green, R. (2007). Podcasts as a Supplement in Tertiary Education: An Experiment with Two Computer Science Courses. *Conference on Mobile Learning Technologies and Applications, February 19, Auckland, NewZealand.*

Bruder, P. The toolbox: Prezi presentations engage and motivate students. *NJEA Review, 84*(6), 30-32.

Bull, G., & Kajder, S. (2004). Digital storytelling in the language arts classroom. *Learning & Leading with Technology, 32*(4), 46-49.

Burden, K. & Atkinson, S. (2008). Evaluating pedagogical 'affordances' of media sharing Web 2.0 technologies: A case study. In Hello! Where are you in the landscape of educational technology? *ascilite, Melbourne, Australia.*

CDS. (2016). *Center for Digital Storytelling*. Retrieved from http://www.storycenter.org

Christenson, C. M., & Raynor, M. E. (2003). *The innovator's solution: Creating and sustaining Successful Growth*. Cambridge, MA: Harvard University Press.

Crosby, C. (2010). Prezi: Shaking off the PowerPoint death grip. *Slaw*. Retrieved from http://www.slaw.ca/2010/10/25/prezi-shaking-off-the-powerpoint-death-grip/

Davis, A., & McGrail, E. (2009). 'Proof-revising' with Podcasting: Keeping Readers in Mind as Students Listen to and Rethink their Writing. *Reading Teacher 62*(6), 522-529.

Hadjioannour, X., & Hutchinson, M. (2014). Fostering Awareness through Transmediation: Preparing Pre-Service Teachers for Critical Engagement with Multicultural Literature. *International Journal of Multicultural Education, 16*(1), 1-20.

Hammersley, B. (2004, February 12). Audible Revolution. *The Guardian*. Retrieved from https://www.theguardian.com/media/2004/feb/12/broadcasting.digitalmedia

Holec, H. (1987). The Learner as Manager: Managing Learning or Managing to learn? In A. Enden, & J. Rubin (Eds.), *Learner Strategies in Language Learning* (pp. 145-156). London: Prentice Hall.

Jenkins, M., & Lonsdale, J. (2007). Evaluating the effectiveness of digital storytelling for student reflection. *ascilite, Singapore*, 440-444.

Lambert, J. (2010). *Digital storytelling cookbook*. Berkley, CA: Digital Diner Press.

Laurillard, D., Stratfold, M., Luckin, R., Plowman, L., & Taylor, J. (2000). Affordances for learning in a non-linear narrative medium. *Journal of Interactive Media in Education, 2*.

Leberecht, T. (2009, August 23). Power to Prezi! *CNet News*. Retrieved from http://news.cnet.com/8301-13641_3-10315737-44.html

Lechlitner, M., Kocain, M., Reitz, K., Stroman, L., Kwon, I., Sheldon, B., Peedin, I., Chalfant, J., Robinson, C., Siebenhausen, N., Towns, W., Boldebuck, M., Applegate, L.,

Cain, B., & Cunningham, A. (2011). Prezi. *Web 2.0 tools - New possibilities for teaching and learning*. Retrieved from https://wiki.itap.purdue.edu/display/INSITE/Prezi

Leimbach, L. (2010). Prezi. Just plain good for content. *Teacher Tech*. Retrieved from http://rsu2teachertech.wordpress.com/2010/11/09/prezi-just-plain-good-for-content/

Liou, H. C., & Peng, S. Y. (2009). Training Effects on Computer-Mediated Peer Review. *System 37*(3), 514-525.Jakes, D. (2009). *Capturing stories, capturing lives: An introduction to digital storytelling*. Retrieved from http://www.jakesonline.org/dstory_ice.pdf

Martin, B. & Carle, E. (1995). *Brown bear, brown bear, what do you see?* Canada: Fitzhenry & Whiteside Ltd.

Mayer, R. E. (2003). The Promise of Multimedia Learning: Using the Same Instructional Design Methods across Different Media. *Learning and Instruction, 13*(2), 125.

Ohler, J. B. (2008). *Digital storytelling in the classroom: New media pathways to literacy, learning, and creativity*. California: Corwin Press.

Peridore, S. & Lines, C. (2011). An online educational framework for second language teaching. In C. Ho & M. Lin (Eds.), *Proceedings of E-Learn: World Conference on E-Learning in Corporate, Government, Healthcare, and Higher Education* 2011 (pp. 365-368). Chesapeake, VA: Association for the Advancement of Computing in Education (AACE).

Pinto Pires, S. (2010). Prezi killed PowerPoint! How to integrate Prezi in the classroom. *e-blahblah*. Retrieved from http://e-blahblah.com/index.php/2010/01/prezi-killed-powerpoint-how-to-integrate-prezi-in-the-classroom/

Potter, N. (2011). Prezi for the win? Ten top tips to make a good one. *the wikiman*. Retrieved from http://thewikiman.org/blog/?p=866

Rhinehart Neas, L. M. (2012). Assessing with PowerPoint and Prezi presentations. *Bright Hub Education*. Retrieved from http://www.brighthub education.com/student-assessment-tools/59411-powerpoint-presentations-as-assessment-tool/

Robin, B. (2008). *The educational uses of digital storytelling - Getting started*. Retrieved from http://digitalstorytelling.coe.uh.edu/getting_started.html

Robin, B. (2016). *About digital storytelling*. Retrieved from http://digitalstorytelling.coe.uh.edu/page.cfm?id=27&cid=27&sublinkid=31

Robin, B. R., & Pierson, M. E. (2005). *A multilevel approach to using digital storytelling in the classroom*. Society for Information Technology & Teacher Education, Phoenix, AZ.

Robinson, S. (2014). Embracing 21st century literacies in the ELA classroom. In J. Vitelli & M. Leikomaa (Eds.), *Proceedings of Edmedia: World Conference on Educational Media and Technology 2014* (pp. 1811-1825). Association for the Advancement of Computing in Education (AACE).

Sabio, R. (2010). Prezi presentations. *EFL and ESL Lesson Plans*. Retrieved from http://www.ralphsesl junction.com/prezi.html

Sampson, D., Karagiannidis, C., Schenone, A., Cardinali, F. (2002). Knowledge-on-demand in e-Learning and e-working Settings. *Educational Technology & Society, 5(2)*.

Schar, S., Schluep, S., Schierz, C., & Krueger, H. (2000). Interaction for computer aided learning. *Interactive Multimedia Electronic Journal of Computer-Enhanced Learning, 2(1)*.

Swinford, E. (2006). *Fixing PowerPoint annoyances: How to fix the most annoying things about your favorite presentation program*. CA: O'Reilly.

Udell, J. (2004, November, 15). Name that Genre. *InfoWorld*. Retrieved from http://jonudell.net/udell/2004-11-15-name-that-genre.html

Watrall, E. (2009). Challenging the presentation paradigm: Prezi. *ProfHacker. Chronicle of Higher Education*. Retrieved from http://chronicle.com/ blogs/profhacker/challenging-the-presentation-paradigm-prezi/22646

Glossary

BYOD	Bring Your Own Device
CMC	Computer Mediated Communication
EFL	English as a Foreign Language
ELA	English Language Arts
ESL	English as a Second Language
ESP	English for Specific Purposes
JIT learning	Just-In-Time learning
JIC learning	Just-In-Case learning
JSON	JavaScript Object Notation
KOD	Knowledge-On-Demand
LMS	Learning Management System
OPML	Outline Processor Markup Language
PLE	Personal Learning Environment
RSS	Really Simple Syndication
TESOL	Teaching English to Speakers of Other Languages
WYSIWYG	What You See Is What You Get
ZUI	Zoomable User Interface

About the Book

Since the turn of the century, emerging technologies, along with their use in educational contexts, have seen a number of radical changes occur within the learner landscape, and these have impacted both teachers and students. This has seen changes in the way that learners engage with content and interact with instructors. Technological advancement has been rapid, and its impact on teaching and learning is ever-constant. This has led to a need for educators to continually assess and consider the implication that new and emerging technologies hold for their teaching contexts, their professional development, and the skills possessed and required by their students. It is here that the value of this book becomes apparent, as practitioners will be able to walk away with a greater understanding of how to best employ various aspects of technology-driven learning, instruction, and assessment techniques when teaching English to speakers of other languages (TESOL) from a variety of pedagogical contexts.

In this book, the use of more 'traditional' software tools and classroom staples are reexamined for educational advantage in the digital era and for use with 21st century learners. Specifically covered topics are: making meaning from experience with digital storytelling, development of interactive multimedia-based presentations with Prezi, and means of supporting and supplementing instruction with podcasts and screencasts. This book is intended to be read in whole or in part by teachers, students, parents, and any other stakeholders who may be interested in the topics.

About the Author

David Kent is an Assistant Professor at the Graduate School of TESOL-MALL at Woosong University in the Republic of Korea. He has been working and teaching in Korea since 1995, and with a Doctorate of Education from Curtin University in Australia, he is a specialist in computer assisted language learning (CALL) and the teaching of English to speakers of other languages (TESOL). He has presented at international conferences, as well as published a number of peer-reviewed journal articles, books, and book chapters in his areas of specialization.

Also by David Kent

A Loanword Approach to the Teaching of
English as a Foreign Language in Korea:
Exploring the Effectiveness of a Multimedia Curriculum

Teaching with Technology
Integrating Technology into the TESOL Classroom

TESOL Strategy Guides
Digital Storytelling
The Prezi Presentation Paradigm
Podcasts and Screencasts

www.ingramcontent.com/pod-product-compliance
Lightning Source LLC
Chambersburg PA
CBHW021222090426
42740CB00006B/338